LUKE 12-24
FOR YOU

MIKE McKINLEY
LUKE 12-24 FOR YOU

thegoodbook
COMPANY

Luke 12 – 24 For You
© Michael McKinley/The Good Book Company, 2017

Published by:
The Good Book Company

Tel (US): 866 244 2165
Tel (UK): 0333 123 0880
Email (US): info@thegoodbook.com
Email (UK): info@thegoodbook.co.uk

Websites:
North America: www.thegoodbook.com
UK: www.thegoodbook.co.uk
Australia: www.thegoodbook.com.au
New Zealand: www.thegoodbook.co.nz

(Hardcover) ISBN: 9781784981129
(Paperback) ISBN: 9781784981112

Design by André Parker

Printed in India

CONTENTS

SERIES PREFACE

Each volume of the *God's Word For You* series takes you to the heart of a book of the Bible, and applies its truths to your heart.

The central aim of each title is to be:

- Bible centered
- Christ glorifying
- Relevantly applied
- Easily readable

You can use *Luke 12 – 24 For You:*

To read. You can simply read from cover to cover, as a book that explains and explores the themes, encouragements and challenges of this part of Scripture.

To feed. You can work through this book as part of your own personal regular devotions, or use it alongside a sermon or Bible-study series at your church. Each chapter is divided into two (or occasionally three) shorter sections, with questions for reflection at the end of each.

To lead. You can use this as a resource to help you teach God's word to others, both in small-group and whole-church settings. You'll find tricky verses or concepts explained using ordinary language, and helpful themes and illustrations along with suggested applications.

These books are not commentaries. They assume no understanding of the original Bible languages, nor a high level of biblical knowledge. Verse references are marked in **bold** so that you can refer to them easily. Any words that are used rarely or differently in everyday language outside the church are marked in gray when they first appear, and are explained in a glossary toward the back. There, you'll also find details of resources you can use alongside this one, in both personal and church life.

Our prayer is that as you read, you'll be struck not by the contents of this book, but by the book it's helping you open up; and that you'll praise not the author of this book, but the One he is pointing you to.

Carl Laferton, Series Editor

For Dave and Brenda Pauken,
with gratitude for all of their friendship,
loyalty, and labors in the gospel.

Bible translations used:

- NIV: New International Version, 2011 translation (this is the version being quoted unless otherwise stated)

- ESV: English Standard Version

INTRODUCTION TO LUKE 12 - 24

Imagine that reading the Gospel of Luke is like climbing a mountain. The first few chapters take us into the lower foothills, introducing us to Jesus and the significance of his ministry. He is the promised Savior, who will reign on the throne of David as King over God's people (Luke 1:32-33; 2:11). His arrival heralds the good news of God's favor for the poor, the oppressed, and the needy (4:18-21).

From that point, we begin our climb in earnest, as Jesus launches his public ministry of healing, exorcism, and teaching. Over the next few chapters we continue our gradual ascent, with Jesus revealing his divine power (4:36; 5:1-11, 24), and explaining both the surprising nature of his kingdom (6:20-49; 7:18-23) and also what is required of someone who desires to be a citizen of it (9:23-24).

The first major peak in our climb comes in chapter 9, where Peter identifies Jesus as "God's Messiah" (v 20). Jesus affirms this confession—but then surprisingly tells his disciples that he will suffer terribly, be killed, and then be raised to life on the third day (v 22). From this point on in Luke's Gospel, everything will be leading us towards Jesus' suffering in Jerusalem: "As the time approached for him to be taken up to heaven, Jesus resolutely set out for Jerusalem" (v 51).

Toward the Final Peak

In this second volume, we join Jesus and the disciples on their long and steady approach toward Jerusalem, on something like a plateau extending from Luke 9 to Luke 19. Along the way, we will encounter some of Jesus' best-known and best-loved parables—stories of incredible love with surprising heroes. We will also see Jesus teaching about the nature of his return and intensifying his preparation for his disciples as the crisis of his crucifixion looms ever larger on the horizon.

In the middle of chapter 19, we will find ourselves at the base of a final grand peak, a foreboding cliff that disappears into the clouds.

As Jesus enters into Jerusalem, the unthinkable begins to unfold with a sense of terrible inevitability—the Lord Jesus is betrayed, arrested, tried, and crucified. Luke's account of these world-changing events is careful, detailed, and often heart-wrenching. But just when the darkness begins to seem overwhelming and our trip seems as if it might have been a terrible mistake, the clouds give way to the glories of the resurrection and the joy of the disciples in knowing that their Lord is alive forever.

Your Guide

Luke is a faithful and sure guide to this difficult terrain. He is writing within the lifetime of eyewitnesses of the events (1:2), has done the hard work of investigating properly all that he has been told by those eyewitnesses (v 3), and has written to his first recipient, and to you, so that "you may know ... certainty" about the birth, life, death, resurrection and ascension of Jesus of Nazareth, the Messiah (v 4).

Luke carefully marks out the path and helps us to see where we ought to set our feet. If you are reading this book but you are not yet a follower of Jesus, then I would encourage you to look closely as you climb this mountain. Consider carefully the purpose and meaning of Jesus' suffering. If there was another way for you to experience God's forgiveness and salvation, why would Jesus have endured all of these things? Also, notice carefully what kind of person rejects Jesus and what kind of person receives him joyfully. People who wanted to cling to their own goodness as the basis of their relationship with God did not find much to be excited about in Jesus' ministry. But people who knew how badly they need mercy and forgiveness found Jesus' teaching and death and resurrection to be good news indeed.

And if you are already a follower of Christ, you will find that much of this section of Luke's Gospel will challenge you. Though we are saved by grace, there may be something of the Pharisee's impulse to self-salvation still remaining in us, which reveals itself in the way that we (mis)treat others. Look carefully at the way that Jesus chose to suffer for you so that you could be forgiven. Allow Luke's account of the Savior's agony on the Mount of Olives, his humiliation before his enemies, and his death as a curse on the cross to humble your pride and inflame your love for Christ. Take full advantage of Jesus' pointed warnings about how we must live in light of his future return in glory so that you can live well now in light of that day.

Expect to be transformed by Jesus as you meet him in his word. And enjoy the certainty that Jesus' kingdom is open, that you have entered into it, and that one day you will experience it in all its glorious fullness.

1. FUTURE PRESENT

Everyone plans their actions in the present based on what they believe the future is likely to hold. A person who thinks that rain is likely to fall will make that belief evident by the fact that they have rolled up the windows of their car. A person who believes that the value of a certain stock is about to rise will act on that belief by investing their money in it.

Toward the end of chapter 9 Luke told us that, "As the time approached for him to be taken up to heaven, Jesus resolutely set out for Jerusalem" (Luke 9:51). The second half of Luke's Gospel unfolds in light of that larger purpose, and each encounter seems to move Jesus closer to his death in Jerusalem. The tone of the second half also shifts noticeably, as Jesus spends more time preparing his disciples for life in the time between his departure and his return in glory and judgment.

In this passage we find Jesus addressing his disciples, and in **12:40*** he gives them a key piece of information about the future: "The Son of Man will come at an hour when you do not expect him." Jesus often referred to himself as "the Son of Man" (e.g. Luke 5:24; 7:34), a term that echoed an Old Testament vision of end-time glory and authority found in Daniel 7:13-14. Here Jesus describes a day when his crucifixion, resurrection, and ascension into heaven will be in the past and he will return to earth. And in the brief teachings about masters and servants that surround Luke **12:40**, Jesus makes it clear that when he returns, it will be in order to bring judgment—blessings for the faithful and punishment for the unfaithful.

---

* All Luke verse references being looked at in each chapter are in **bold**.

Good and Bad Servants

In **verses 36-38**, Jesus describes the reward that servants might receive for their **diligence*** while waiting for their master to return. If a master returned to his home after the household had gone to bed (**verse 38** imagines an arrival that took place in the middle of the night or toward daybreak) and with no advance warning (remember, this was a world without phones and email), he would be very pleased to find that his servants were awake and waiting for him. The fact that they were keeping watch for their master even when they had no special reason to expect his return at that moment testified to the fact that they were loyal servants. This kind of servant would receive a most unusual reward—the master himself would take their role, seat them at his table, and serve them himself (**v 37**). The master's return will be good for servants who are "caught" being faithful.

Another example (**v 42-44**) deals not with servants in general but with one in particular who is appointed as a manager. This manager is placed in charge of the master's servants, specifically to provide food for them at the proper time (**v 42**). When the master returns and finds the manager fulfilling his appointed role, "it will be good for that servant" (**v 43**); the master will respond to his servant's faithfulness by putting him charge of everything that he owns. While this principle applies broadly, we should note that it serves as a reminder for those who would serve as leaders in Christ's church. Pastors are servants of Christ who are also managers, charged to provide spiritual food for their fellow servants. They are to discharge their duties faithfully until Christ returns, at which point "it will be good" for them.

Not all servants are rewarded for the way that they conduct themselves, however. Instead of faithfully waiting for their master's return, the servant described in **verses 45-46** responds to the uncertainty surrounding the timing of their master's return by beating the servants and stuffing themselves with food and drink. When the master returns unexpectedly (**v 46**), the punishment he metes out is even more

---

* Words in **gray** are defined in the Glossary (page 191).

shocking than the reward described in **verse 37**: the master will cut the servant to pieces. This expression should mostly likely be understood to represent **figuratively** some kind of extremely severe punishment; if it were meant **literally**, it is hard to understand how the servant could be assigned "a place with the unbelievers." To be placed with unbelievers (the Greek word is literally "faithless") is an appropriate result for a servant who has been unfaithful to his master. The punishment for this servant is total rejection by his returned master.

A Matter of Faithfulness

The meaning of these **parables** does not lie far beneath the surface: following his crucifixion and resurrection, Jesus would ascend into heaven for a time. When he returns, he will reward or punish his servants based on their faithfulness to him during the time that he was not physically present. What is less clear is whom the servants in the parables represent. In **verse 41**, Peter asks whether Jesus intends these teachings for "us" (that is, the disciples mentioned in verse 22) or more broadly for "everyone" (both **professing believers** and unbelievers). Jesus does not answer the question directly, but in response he contrasts a "faithful" manager (**v 42**) and a servant who winds up placed with the "unbelievers" (**v 46**, literally the "faithless").

In the following verses, Jesus introduces a distinction between a servant who knows their master's will but chooses not to do it (**v 47**) and one who earns punishment for themselves without knowing any better (**v 48**). The former might be characterized as professing Christians (especially leaders) who know Jesus' will but choose not to obey it; they will be "beaten with many blows." The latter are unbelievers; they are servants of Jesus as well, no less obligated to serve the one who is indisputably the master of all people in all places. But they do not know how to do so and thus their punishment will be relatively less. In the end, it is a matter of stewardship; much will be expected from the one who has been entrusted with knowledge and given responsibility for Christ's servants. Others are still obligated to serve Jesus, but their responsibility is relatively less.

It may seem hard to reconcile Jesus' words here with the message of grace and forgiveness that is at the heart of the **gospel** message. It is certainly true that when Jesus returns, the only hope that any of us have is located in Christ's mercy and forgiveness, not in our own merit. It is his faithfulness that saves us, not our own. And believers in Christ never need to fear that they might be condemned in the final judgment (see John 5:24).

> Jesus never allows us to separate our trust in him from our obedience to him.

But Jesus never allows us to separate our trust in him from our obedience to him (see Luke 6:43-46); following Jesus' commands is a mark that distinguishes a true believer from someone who merely pays lip service to Jesus as his or her master. A servant who is fundamentally disobedient is a faithless (or unbelieving) servant. Faithful servants can anticipate their master's pleasure and gracious reward (see Matthew 25:23); faithless servants can expect only punishment (see Matthew 25:45-46).

Don't Know When

These parables serve as both an encouragement and a warning, and at their heart is the dynamic of a master's surprise return (Luke **12:38** and **v 46**). It is easy to do what is right when you know that you will be held accountable for your actions, but real faithfulness and integrity are demonstrated by doing right even when it does not seem that there will be consequences for doing wrong. The servants show their true colors by how they act when they do not expect their master's return. In the same way, when the Son of Man returns at an hour that we do not expect (**v 40**), his servants' true colors will be revealed.

There is a tension in the New Testament regarding the timing of Jesus' return. It is clear that we cannot know when it will occur; during his time on earth even Jesus himself did not know the when the time would come (Mark 13:32-33). Various **cults** and false prophets have claimed to know when Jesus would return, but Christians should not be deceived. The Son of Man will return at an hour when we do not expect him.

But on the other side of the tension is the New Testament's witness that there will be certain observable events that will take place before Jesus returns. Later on in Luke's Gospel we read of signs in the heavens that will serve as evidence that the time for Jesus' return has come:

> "There will be signs in the sun, moon and stars. On the earth, nations will be in anguish and perplexity at the roaring and tossing of the sea. People will faint from terror, apprehensive of what is coming on the world, for the heavenly bodies will be shaken. At that time they will see the Son of Man coming in a cloud with power and great glory. When these things begin to take place, stand up and lift up your heads, because your **redemption** is drawing near." (Luke 21:25-28)

It may require wisdom to know which events are being referred to by those signs, but what is clear is that there are things that must occur before Jesus returns (for other examples, see Mark 13:10 and 2 Thessalonians 2:3-4). So we can say that certain signs will precede Jesus' return, and yet it will happen suddenly and in a way that defies our attempts to pinpoint an exact time.

(For a more complete examination of the biblical data, see Wayne Grudem's *Systematic Theology*, pages 1091-1105. You may not necessarily agree with all of Dr. Grudem's conclusions, but you'll benefit from the careful consideration of the relevant biblical texts.)

Therefore, Be Ready

All of Jesus' teaching here is aimed at producing a response in his hearer. Knowledge of the future changes the way we live in the present. If a homeowner knew when the thief was planning to break into his house, he would stay home and thwart the robbery (Luke **12:39**). In the same way, since we have been forewarned that Jesus will return at a time when we do not expect him, we ought to take appropriate measures to make sure that we are among those who are rewarded, and not among those who are cut to pieces and numbered among the unbelievers.

Those measures are described in **verse 35**, where Jesus tells his disciples to "be dressed ready for service" (literally, "your loins are to be girded ready for service"). Much as a modern-day workman might lace up his boots and roll up his sleeves before a day on the jobsite, people in the ancient world would tuck up their flowing garments in order to engage in hard work (there may well be an allusion here to the commandment given to the Israelites in Exodus 12:11). In the same way, in Luke **12:35** the disciples are instructed to "keep your lamps burning." Oil lamps were put out at bedtime in order to save fuel; only someone keeping an alert watch would leave their lamp burning all night. That sort of vigilance and preparedness is the only proper response to the fact that Jesus will return suddenly.

Jesus leaves it up to his hearers to discern what preparedness looks like. But in the context of Luke's Gospel, we might speculate as to some of the behaviors that comprise the faithfulness that Jesus will reward. These might include:

- fear of the Lord (v 5)

- boldness in witness (v 8-9)

- radical generosity (v 33)

- care for fellow believers (**v 42-43**)

- general obedience to the commands of the Lord (**v 47**)

Jesus' teaching is meant to elicit a response like that of Jonathan Edwards, who, when he was a young man, made this resolution:

"Resolved, never to do any thing which I should be afraid to do if I expected it would not be above an hour before I should hear the last trump."

(*The Works of Jonathan Edwards, Volume One*, page 21)

Questions for reflection

1. What do your present actions suggest you truly believe about the future, and the extent to which Jesus' return affects those beliefs?

2. "Faithful servants can anticipate their master's pleasure and gracious reward." What does this motivate you to do in your Master's service today?

3. Is there a temptation to disobedience you regularly give in to, which you could resist by saying to yourself, "Be dressed ready for service"?

PART TWO

Surprising Words

In Luke **12:51**, Jesus asks **rhetorically** if the disciples think that he came to bring peace on earth. He quickly dispels any such notion, but perhaps we can understand why some of his disciples might have gotten the wrong impression. After all, the angels had responded to the birth of Jesus with a declaration of peace on earth (2:14), and the prophet Isaiah had spoken of the one who would come as the Prince of Peace (Isaiah 9:6). Jesus himself said that he was leaving his own unique peace with his disciples (John 14:27), and the **apostle** Peter was able to summarize the gospel message as "the good news of peace through Jesus Christ" (Acts 10:36).

But **Simeon** had already seen that the child Jesus was "destined to cause the falling and rising of many in Israel, and to be a sign that will be spoken against, so that the thoughts of many hearts will be revealed" (Luke 2:34-35). And even the angels that appeared to the shepherds had acknowledged that the peace that would come with the arrival of Jesus was not one that would be spread out universally among all people. It was particularly for those "on whom [God's] favor rests" (2:14).

That assumed distinction between the world as a whole and those specific people on whom God's favor rests may help us to understand Jesus' startling teaching here. The coming of Jesus would result in a fundamental separation on earth (**12:51**), and the clear implication is that this separation would be based on whether people received or rejected the message and person of Jesus. This division was so powerful that it even would break apart the most tightly unified human institution: the family. For example, a family of five would be split, with two of its members now opposed to the other three (**v 52**). Because of the arrival of Jesus, relationships that God created to be intensely intimate (fathers and sons, mothers and daughters, etc.) now would be characterized by opposition and antagonism (**v 53**). What accounts for this surprising division, and how can we understand that it would not merely be an accident of Jesus' coming but rather the point of it?

Fire and Baptism

In **verse 49**, Jesus says that he has come to "bring fire on the earth." **John the Baptist** had used fire as a picture of the way that the one who was coming would bring judgment and the purging of evil (3:9, 17), and certainly that judgment would come in a full way at the second coming of Christ (remember 12:45-48). It is most likely this end-time fire that Jesus longed to kindle, since it would establish God's righteous kingdom in a final way. But we can say that the division that Jesus speaks of in **verses 51-53**—that split which will naturally occur between those who receive the message of Jesus with joy and those who reject him—amounts to a preliminary experience of that end-time fire. When family members divide along the lines of their response to Jesus, it reveals which of them are those on whom the favor of God rests. The division demonstrates who are the faithful servants and who will be taken away in the fire of end-time judgment. The new spiritual distinction between people will result even in opposition within families.

In **verse 50**, Jesus speaks of a baptism that he has yet to undergo, making it clear that he is not referring to his baptism in the Jordan by John. The image of being plunged beneath the waters in baptism can be understood as a symbolic picture of God's judgment. In the Greek translation of the Old Testament, the text of Job 9:31 uses a form of the word *bapto* to describe the way that Job believes that God will plunge him into a pit. In certain places in the Old Testament, God's judgment is pictured as a flood of overwhelming water (see Isaiah 8:7-8 and Jonah 2:3-6). Darrell Bock puts it this way:

> "Thus the point of the **metaphor** is that Jesus faces a period of being uniquely inundated with God's judgment, an allusion to rejection and persecution." (*Luke 9:51 –24:53*, page 1194)

When Jesus speaks of his upcoming baptism, he is referring to his crucifixion and all of the events that lead up to it.

In Luke **12:49-50** Jesus expresses a strong desire for these events to take place. He wishes that the fire of judgment "were already kindled," and he feels that he is under constraint until his baptism is completed. Luke has told us already that Jesus has set his face towards Jerusalem (9:51), where he will endure the judgment of God on the cross. Jesus is constrained by his understanding of the two-fold mission on which his Father has sent him—a mission which corresponds to the division that he brings. On one hand, for those who reject him the result of Jesus' coming will be the fires of divine judgment. But on the other hand, Jesus will himself experience the flood of God's **wrath** on the cross for those on the other side of the divide, those who receive him in faith.

Good Division?

Ours is an age that prizes tolerance and inclusion, and the Bible itself commends unity in many places (e.g. Psalm 133:1; Acts 4:32; Ephesians 4:3). In that light, Jesus' passion for division here can be shocking. But there is a sense in which the Bible is all about making a division between people. From the very beginning, there has been a bright line marking off the people of God from the people who are in rebellion against him. People were either in the ark built by Noah or they were outside of it. People were either **circumcised** members of Abraham's family or they were cut off from God's people (see Genesis 17:10-14). Even now, people are either members of God's household or are foreigners and strangers (see Ephesians 2:19).

In that light, it is easier to understand why Jesus' arrival can be cast in terms of setting people against each other. People who reject him and his message place themselves in opposition to God himself (Luke 10:16). And so the division that Jesus brings is simply an inevitable separation between sheep and goats (Matthew 25:31-33), between those who belong to the light and those who walk in darkness

(1 Thessalonians 5:4-9). If this makes us uncomfortable, it is likely because our understanding of Jesus is unbalanced.

David Tiede is correct when he says:

"Those who would reduce Jesus to a sentimental savior of a doting God have not come to terms with the depth of divine passion, of the wrath and love of God which is revealed in Jesus' word, will, and obedience even unto death."

(Quoted in Bock, *Luke 9:51 – 24:53*, page 1196)

If we would be faithful to Jesus, we must be willing to embrace the separation that he brings. In some denominations it is fashionable to argue in the name of unity that Christians should remain in churches even after they have abandoned the gospel and embraced **theological** positions that contradict the Bible's clear teaching. But Jesus seems to know nothing of unity that is not rooted in a genuine faith in him and his truth (see John 17:20-23).

So many definitions in this world

> Jesus knows nothing of unity that is not rooted in a genuine faith in him.

We must not miss how extraordinary Jesus' teaching here really is. Teachers do not normally claim priority over family relationships, but Jesus does. There are many places in the world where a person's decision to follow Christ means that they will be cut off by and from their families. In other places, one person's decision to follow Christ may introduce awkwardness into the life of a family or tension into a marriage. Those things are very difficult to deal with, but none of them constitute legitimate grounds for not following Jesus. We simply cannot hold any loyalty above our loyalty to Christ; he is no ordinary teacher and his disciples may have to pay a very high price in order to follow him.

Read the Signs

Jesus' attention moves from the disciples, where it has been ever since Luke 12:22, to "the crowd" (**v 54**) of "hypocrites" (as he calls them in **v 56**). The people were adept at reading the signs of "the earth and the sky" when they pointed to a change of weather; a cloud in the west would bring heavy moisture from the Mediterranean Sea and frequently result in a rainstorm (**v 54**). Wind from the south would travel over the desert regions and normally indicated the arrival of high temperatures (**v 55**). But in light of their aptitude for discerning the significance of certain meteorological indicators, Jesus wonders at their inability to "interpret this present time" (**v 56**).

The word translated as "time" (*kairon*) has the sense of an opportunity that has been presented, or a season that has begun but will only last a certain amount of time. Jesus had come, bringing the **kingdom of God** with him and giving clear evidence of God's work through him, but most of the people had ignored the signs. Thus, the members of the crowd were not "hypocrites" in the sense that we normally give to the word (someone who says one thing but intentionally does another), but rather ,because they gave the outward impression of being people who understood the world around them when in fact they had no clue about the important things that were taking place in their midst. The rebuking tone that Jesus takes with them indicates that this failure to understand, "more a problem of the will than anything else" (Edwards, *The Gospel According to Luke*, page 387).

The remedy for the crowd's failure to interpret the season of Christ's arrival is to "judge for yourselves what is right" (**v 57**). And in order to illustrate the importance of acting in light of the pressing reality of the moment, Jesus presents them with a **hypothetical** situation in **verse 58**: imagine you and an adversary are going before a magistrate in order that a financial dispute can be settled. That magistrate might send the matter to a judge, and if the judge decides the case in your opponent's favor, the consequences are dire:

you will be imprisoned until your debt is paid. In such a scenario, any person with a bit of common sense will interpret the situation accurately and take action to prevent the potential disaster. He will "try hard to be reconciled on the way" and thus prevent the matter from ever reaching the point of a condemning judgment (**v 59**). Just as they were able to read the signs that indicated the coming weather, in the same way the crowds demonstrated a kind of wisdom in their personal and financial affairs. No one with a good head on their shoulders would let a dispute escalate to the point where they would face condemning judgment.

Many of us would do well to heed Jesus' practical advice, for when conflicts escalate there is rarely a satisfactory resolution. It is the way of wisdom to make peace before things get out of hand, and it brings the name of Jesus into disrepute when Christians cannot resolve their differences without involving civil authorities (see 1 Corinthians 6:1-8). It is much better to make peace before you have to pay the price for your offenses.

If that is true in human interaction, it is even more so when we consider our relationship with God. Just as we should be reconciled with our opponents before it is too late, so Jesus is urging the crowds to show common sense by being reconciled to God during this time of his ministry among them. If Jesus has in fact come to bring fire to the earth (Luke **12:49**), then it would be wise to be reconciled to God (the ultimate judge) before it is too late. Sin has left each one of us with a debt toward God that we cannot repay (remember the imagery of 7:41-49). But the coming of Jesus signifies that we are in a time when we can still be reconciled to God through him. There will be a time when it is to late and the judgment against us will have been rendered. The warning to us is clear: do not delay! Do not miss out on the time to be made right with God.

Questions for reflection

1. To whom are Jesus' words here on the family and division a reassurance? To whom would they be a challenge?

2. Have you witnessed unfaithful unity? Have you witnessed unhelpful division? What principles can help us navigate these difficult judgments without making either error, do you think?

3. Have Jesus' words here reshaped your view of him in any way? How?

2. DEATH COMES AND THE KINGDOM GROWS

The theme of the sudden, unexpected approach of judgment carries over from Luke 12 into Jesus' teaching in chapter 13. Some people who were present informed Jesus about "the Galileans whose blood Pilate had mixed with their **sacrifices**" (**13:1**). There is no certain record of this action of Pontius Pilate, the Roman governor of the province of Judea, in history (though see Bock, *Luke 9:51 – 24:53*, page 1205 for a summary of different possibilities); but the specific details of what happened are not required to understand what is happening in this passage. Jesus has been talking about interpreting the times (12:54-59), and it seems that some in the crowd wondered if this outrageous act of violence had a larger significance. The masses had high hopes for Jesus as a political and even military deliverer (see John 6:15); it could well be that they expected Jesus to do something to avenge the dead or make a move to protect his fellow countrymen in the future.

Jesus, however, takes an opportunity to press home a spiritual principle. When disaster strikes, we often derive comfort from some sort of explanation for why it occurred. If we can explain why it happened, then we can provide ourselves with reasons why it will not happen to us. And so perhaps these Galileans died because they were "worse sinners than all the other Galileans" (Luke **13:2**). Perhaps this was God's swift judgment coming on them; maybe Pilate's actions were really a form God's judgment against their evil.

In **verse 4**, Jesus presents them with another example: the death of eighteen residents of Jerusalem on whom a tower fell, another incident that was apparently well known to his hearers but has been lost to history. And again Jesus questions them about the reason for the tragedy; were the victims "more guilty than all the others living in Jerusalem"?

The question that Jesus asks gets right to the heart of one of the great mysteries of human existence: why do bad things happen? The Bible's answer to that question is not simplistic; the book of Job represents an exploration of many of the potential reasons why suffering might come to an individual's life. But what is clear is that we cannot look at any one disaster or tragedy and presume to know God's larger purpose. Sometimes God sends suffering in direct response to sin (see Psalm 32:3-4). In other cases he sends pain in order to reveal himself to the person who is suffering (see the explanation for the man's blindness in John 9 and the end result

> When we see suffering, we need to resist the urge to draw rapid conclusions about God's purpose.

in the man's life). Sometimes he intends for difficulty to help prevent sin from taking root in someone's life (see 2 Corinthians 12:7; 1 Peter 4:1-3). When we see suffering in our lives or in the world around us, we need to resist the urge to draw rapid and unfounded conclusions about God's purpose in sending it.

But in the two specific cases that Jesus raises in Luke 13, he does in fact know the reason. The answer to Jesus' questions about whether these tragedies were a response to the sin of the victims is the same in both cases: "I tell you, no!" (Luke **13:3, 5**). Instead of hiding behind the pretense that these kinds of things only happen to the worst kind of people, Jesus warns them that unless they repent the same thing will happen to them. Now, Jesus obviously is not saying that his hearers will experience the exact same fate as those unfortunate people who were slaughtered by Pilate or crushed under a tower. Rather, his point seems to be that the people who died suddenly never had a chance to repent at the end of their lives. Repentance involves both a change of heart and a change of life; when someone repents they feel remorse for their sin and they turn toward God in a desire to obey him. If these Galileans had not repented of their sins, they would have faced God's judgment unprepared. These tragedies were intended to lead Jesus' hearers to repentance.

In that sense, this is a variation on the theme of chapter 12—Jesus could come back at any moment or you could die at any second. That is simply the reality of human life; tragedies remind us that we are not guaranteed tomorrow. There is nothing to say that the building you sit in at this moment will not collapse in one minute's time, ending your life and bringing you before God to give an account for your life. And so in light of that reality in Luke **13:3** and **5**, Jesus warns his hearers to repent.

The Fruitless Fig Tree

In order to illustrate that call to repentance, the Lord tells a parable in **verses 6-9**. The flow of the story is fairly easy to understand. It begins with a fig tree growing in a vineyard. That might seem odd since we normally associate vineyards with grapes instead of figs, but the soil in a vineyard was suitable for figs and the fig trees were often used to help hold the grape vines off the ground. The tree in question has not produced any fruit in its first three years, however, and so the owner orders that it be cut down lest it continue to use up perfectly good soil (**v 6-7**). The vinedresser intercedes on behalf of the tree, asking for another year to try and coax fruit from it by loosening the soil around it and fertilizing it well (**v 8**). But in the end, he concedes that if the tree continues to be unfruitful through the following year, it should be cut down (**v 9**).

In his parable, Jesus is reiterating his warning from **verses 3** and **5** to the nation of Israel in general and to his hearers in particular—unless you repent, you too will all perish. The Old Testament used the image of a fig tree to represent Israel (e.g. Joel 1:7), and we should read this parable in that light. The fig tree was given another year to produce fruit before it was cut down, but the reader is left without much hope that the extra time will result in a drastic change in the tree's fruitfulness. In the same way, the nation of Israel was in a season where God's judgment had been delayed, but not indefinitely so. And so Jesus calls them to repent—to "bear fruit" in the language of the parable—before God sends his judgment on them. Sadly, history tells us that this warning went largely unheeded by Jesus' hearers. In AD 70, judgment did fall on Israel like so many towers as the Romans swept in, Jerusalem was leveled and the nation was largely destroyed.

But we should not allow the distance of time and culture to make us miss the fact that Jesus' warning applies to us as well. There is a coming day on which you will be called to give an account for the fruitlessness in your life and, like the two examples in Luke **13:1-5**, you may not get advanced notice of when disaster is about to fall upon you (or, to put it in terms of chapter 12, you may not get advance notice of when the master will return and evaluate your service to him).

That might seem like an unpleasant message, and perhaps even a repetitive one in light of Jesus' teaching in chapter 12. But while the examples of the slaughter of the Galileans and the collapse of the tower emphasize the suddenness of God's judgment, the parable of the fig tree reminds us that God is more patient with us than we have a right to expect. Every man, woman, and child on earth deserves God's judgment against his or her sin. The fact that life continues day after day means that God is extraordinarily merciful to and patient with everyone. And so we are like the fig tree after the owner's first visit. The standards of God's holiness and justice find the fruit of our lives lacking; the question for us is: will the mercy and patience of God lead us to repent?

The call to repentance is both bad news and good news. On the one hand, the bad news: repentance involves an admission of guilt on our part. It involves saying the same thing about your life that God says about it—that you are the tree without all the fruit that you should have, even that you deserve to have a tower fall on your head because of your sins. That is the opposite of the way that most of us feel about

> The fact that life continues day after day means that God is extremely patient.

our lives; we normally feel that we deserve better than any kind of suffering. Repentance involves realizing that God does not owe you anything except judgment for your sin.

Here in Luke 13, Jesus is saying in effect, *When you hear about people being killed by Pilate or by falling towers, let that lead you to repentance. Don't look at them and think, "They must have been the worst kind of sinners." Instead, think, "Because of my sin, I deserve a fate worse than that." Let that thought lead you to repentance for your sins.*

But the good news of repentance is that God is merciful, patient, and willing to forgive. In Jesus' parable, the tree deserves to be destroyed. It is using up resources but not producing any fruit (**v 7**). And when the vinedresser intercedes for it, he asks for a reprieve, an opportunity for the tree to become fruitful. But notice that he doesn't argue for the tree's worthiness; the vinedresser does not suggest to the owner that his standards are too high or that there really is fruit present that the owner is not seeing. Instead, the vinedresser pleads for patience and an opportunity for the tree to amend its ways.

That is a picture of God's great love and patience. There is nothing in a sinner that deserves forgiveness; God would be well within the bounds of justice had he destroyed any sinner. But in his own great mercy God often withholds his judgment and allows time for repentance. The apostles made this same connection between the delay of God's judgment and our need to repent. Decades after Jesus told this parable of the fruitless tree, Peter reflected on the reason why Jesus had not returned from heaven to judge the world and bring his people to heaven: "The Lord is not slow in keeping his promise, as some understand slowness. Instead he is patient with you, not wanting anyone to perish, but everyone to come to repentance" (2 Peter 3:9). And the apostle Paul could ask people who trusted in their own goodness: "Do you show contempt for the riches of his kindness, forbearance and patience, not realizing that God's kindness is intended to lead you to repentance?" (Romans 2 v 4).

Questions for reflection

1. "Why would God allow suffering?" How could you use these verses as part of an answer to that question?

2. "Why hasn't Jesus returned yet?" How could you use these verses as part of an answer to that question?

3. How will these verses help you next time you are watching the news and it features a report about death?

PART TWO

Luke bookends the next section of his Gospel with accounts of two miraculous healings. In Luke **13:11** we are introduced to a woman "who had been crippled by a spirit for eighteen years." **Demonic** affliction in the New Testament often manifested itself through physical suffering (e.g. Matthew 12:22), and in this woman's case she was "bent over and could not straighten up at all." The long duration of her suffering makes her situation all the more pitiable and Jesus' healing power all the more startling. The terrible oppression of an evil spirit had defined this woman's life for almost two decades, but Jesus' power and authority is such that he can set her free from her infirmity (Luke **13:12**) with a touch of his hands (**v 13**). For her part, the woman knows that Jesus' ministry represents the work of God, and so she knows to whom she should offer praise once she is able to straighten up (**v 13**).

Then in **14:2**, we read about a man who had dropsy, an often painful condition where tissues in the body swell with excess fluid (now commonly referred to as edema). Unlike the bent-over woman in the synagogue, there is no indication that this man's condition is the result of direct demonic influence. Luke reports the healing simply and with a minimum of detail, merely telling us that Jesus took him and healed him and sent him away (**v 4**).

The Question of the Sabbath

The power and compassion of Jesus is on clear display in both healings, but there is actually a much larger issue at stake in these events. The setting for each miracle is the Sabbath (**13:10** and **14:1**), a day when the people of Israel had been instructed by the Lord to rest from their labors. Jesus' act of healing on the Sabbath brought him into conflict with the scruples of the religious leaders, who seemed to believe that healing constituted work that was unlawful on the Sabbath. And so we wind up with a pair of disconnects that would be funny if they were not so sad: a woman is released from demonic oppression but the **synagogue** leader is indignant and scolds the crowd for not coming to get healed some other day (**13:14**); similarly, the prospect of healing a sick man is met with the stony silence of the religious leaders (**14:4**). This conflict seems to be exactly Jesus' intention, for in each case he is the one driving the action. He saw the afflicted woman and called her over to himself (**13:2**). He himself initiated the conversation about whether or not it would be appropriate to heal the sick man on the Sabbath (**14:3**).

Jesus' ministry blesses the two people who are healed, but it also serves to highlight the hypocrisy of his opponents. They imagine that they are the ones who love the law of God, but they are criticizing him for doing something that is obviously in keeping with the purpose and spirit of God's law. Jesus demonstrates their hypocrisy by pointing to the way they treat their animals—surely they do not allow their animals to dehydrate and go hungry just because it is the Sabbath (**13:15**). Their actions betray the fact that they understand that the law regarding the Sabbath was never intended to create or perpetuate suffering. If it is permissible to care for a donkey on the Sabbath, how much more is it permissible to heal "a daughter of Abraham" who has been suffering for so long at the hand of Satan (**v 16**)? They end up humiliated by their own hypocrisy, unable to see Jesus' actions as "wonderful" (**v 17**).

The healing of the man with dropsy took place in a similar environment of distrust and suspicion; Luke tells us that Jesus was being "carefully watched" in the home of a prominent **Pharisee** (**14:1**). Jesus may well have had a reputation for performing acts of mercy on the Sabbath by this point, and his opponents were looking for a reason to criticize him. In **verse 3**, Jesus presses home the question that everyone is asking: Is it lawful to heal on the Sabbath or not? His opponents refuse to go on the record with a response, but Jesus' actions make his answer clear. And just as he did in chapter 13, he demonstrates the hypocrisy of those who would pit God's law against God's mercy: *If one of you has a child or an ox that falls into a well on* *the Sabbath day, will you not immediately pull it out* (**14:5**)? Again, the exposing of their hypocrisy silences Jesus' opponents (**v 6**).

We might not relate to the way that the Pharisees zealously guarded the observance of the Sabbath, but there might be some things in our own lives that have become so important to us that we miss out on what God is doing around us. Church programs, personal disciplines, and styles of music may be all well and good. But if they prevent us from showing mercy to those in need or helping others to grow in Christ, then we have to ask whether the Lord would have us reorder our priorities.

The Kingdom that Grows

The Greek text of **13:18** contains the word "therefore" (*oun*), which helps us to interpret Jesus' words in **verses 18-21** in light of the healing that came immediately before them. The demonstration of power that could deliver the bent-over woman from the power of Satan has in **verse 3** and **verse 5** raised the question that Jesus picks up in both **verse 18** and **verse 20**: if Jesus is establishing the kingdom of God, what will it look like? Will it be characterized by spectacular displays of spiritual might? Will there be a military and political conquest attached to it?

Jesus' answers might not be what we would expect initially: the kingdom of God is like a mustard seed planted by a man in his garden (**v 19**) and like yeast mixed into about 60 pounds (30 kg) of flour (**v 21**). Each of those examples puts in our minds something that might seem small and insignificant, but will ultimately grow to have an extensive impact. A tiny little mustard seed can grow to be an impressive tree that can shelter birds. A small bit of leaven (yeast) can have a massive influence, leavening all of a large batch of dough.

That is what the kingdom of God is like. Its beginnings may not be impressive to the Pharisees and the rulers of the synagogues. A woman who can now stand up straight, a man whose limbs are no longer filled with fluid—those things might seem like mere drops of water

> If you give the kingdom of God time, it will change everything.

in the comprehensive ocean of human suffering. How can that be the kingdom of God? But if you give it time, it will change everything. It will grow and spread like a tree. It will transform everything, like yeast in dough. That is the way the kingdom of God will work. It does not work like the kingdoms of the world, which rise to power suddenly and spectacularly only to fade from the scene in a relative blink of the eye. Instead, it grows slowly and imperceptibly until it has achieved incredible influence.

The history of the church serves as an illustration of Jesus' teaching. In the book of Acts we see a small band of disciples grow to the point where people from every nation on earth are able to "[perch] in its branches." The message about Jesus spreads slowly but inexorably until it has reached every part of the map, leavening the entire lump of the world. The very existence of our faith, separated as we are from Jesus' earthly ministry by great distance and time, gives evidence for what Jesus is teaching. It is the way of God to begin something great in small and unimpressive ways that confound human expectations and vanity (see 1 Corinthians 1:18-31). Though the beginnings may seem humble and the growth may seem small, nothing can stop the kingdom of God from spreading through the whole world. Though the opponents of the church may seems fierce and powerful, nothing will prevent Jesus' kingdom from growing.

This should be an encouragement to us when it does not seem that God is at work in the world around us. When we share the gospel but do not see immediate fruit, we have to remember that God works in his own ways and in his own timing (see 1 Corinthians 3:6-7). When our churches and our daily lives seem ordinary and unspectacular, we should take comfort from the lesson of the mustard seed—God does not often work in ways that seem impressive at the beginning. We can continue being faithful, knowing that God is in no hurry and that he is content to build patiently and slowly.

A Lot or a Few?

The events recorded in Luke 13:22-35 do not necessarily follow **chronologically** from those of the previous passage. In fact, **verse 22** seems to indicate that some time has passed since the conclusion of **verse 21** as Jesus traveled around the region teaching. But the question posed in **verse 23** does seem to indicate that Jesus' warnings about judgment and division have touched a nerve, and so someone asks, *Will those who are saved be few?* Is Jesus saying that something less than all of Israel is going to take part in the redemption of the **Messiah**?

Jesus does not answer the question directly, but the two illustrations that he uses to speak about salvation are sobering. First, he says that it is entered through a narrow door (**v 24**). Contrary to the common religious pluralism of our day, which likes to imagine that the many religions of the world represent different paths to the same salvation, Jesus teaches that the only way into salvation is through a proper response to him and his teaching. It is a narrow door, not one that a person would go through casually or accidentally.

Not only is salvation like a narrow door, but it is a door that will one day be permanently shut (**v 25**), cutting off anyone who is not already inside. The opportunity to respond to the message of Jesus was fleeting for the people in that day, because Jesus was making his way to Jerusalem (**v 22**), where he would be executed. The crowds might be taking comfort from the fact that they are eating and drinking with Jesus and that he is teaching in their streets (**v 26**); they might imagine that this indicates that they are on the inside of his salvation. But unless they respond to his message of repentance (v 5), he will disavow any knowledge of them (**v 25** and **v 27**).

For us, the urgency of Jesus' message comes from the certainty of our death and the possibility that Jesus might return in our lifetime. In the terms of Jesus' response, these events have the effect of closing the door of salvation. There will come a day when it is too late and there will no longer be an opportunity to respond to Jesus' message.

But it is not too late right now; at this moment, anyone who knocks on the door will have it opened to them (11:9).

Jesus does not force his hearers to guess about the proper response to his warning; in **13:24** the command is to "make every effort to enter through the narrow door." The sense of the Greek word that Luke uses (*agonizesthe*) has the sense of intense exertion toward a goal. We cannot take for granted that we have entered into God's salvation, but we must invest all of our energy in making sure that we are through that door before it is too late. We should not misunderstand Jesus as saying that we must strive to pile up good works that will merit passage through the door. Instead, the point is to "labor hard at listening and responding to his message" (Bock, *Luke 9:51 – 24:53*, page 1234).

Unexpected Guests

If Jesus' audience found it surprising that the door of salvation was narrow and likely to close at any moment, they were probably even more surprised to find out who would make it through the door and who would not. The Jewish nation took great comfort from the fact that they were God's people; after all, they had access to God's word and all of the promises of God made to the **patriarchs** (see that assumption being addressed by John's words in Luke 3:8; see also Romans 3:1-2). But in Luke **13:28** Jesus seeks to undermine their self-confidence—they will experience great sorrow and pain ("weeping" and "gnashing of teeth") when they find themselves "thrown out," left to gaze in on their beloved patriarchs and prophets enjoying the great feast that would celebrate the ultimate coming of the kingdom of God (see Isaiah 25:6-9 for the Old Testament roots of this image).

The shock of their exclusion will be compounded by the sight of non-Jews—people from "east and west and north and south" (Luke **13:29**)—taking their place at the great celebration. The coming of Jesus reverses human expectations. The people of God are not those who are born to a certain nation, but rather, they are those who receive God's Son with faith (see Romans 2:28-29). The first will now be last, and the last will be first (Luke **13:30**); the insiders have traded places with the outsiders. We must make every effort to ensure that we make it through the door and into the great celebration!

Nothing New

Luke has already given us an indication that Herod Antipas is going to be a problem. He had beheaded John the Baptist (9:9) and was per-plexed by the meaning of Jesus and his ministry (9:7-8); he will also appear later in the passion narrative (23:7-12). But for now, some of the Pharisees warn Jesus that Herod wants to kill him (**13:31**). It is not clear whether these particular Pharisees were motivated by a benevolent de-sire to protect Jesus or whether they simply could not resist an opportu-nity to frustrate one of Herod's plans. Jesus, for his part, dismisses Herod as a "fox" and vows to continue the God-given mission of driving out demons and healing people (**v 32**) that will ultimately culminate in his crucifixion and resurrection "on the third day." Jesus would in fact leave the area where Herod has authority and head to Jerusalem, but not because he was fleeing his treachery. Instead he "must press on today and tomorrow and the next day" (**v 33**), an expression that is "a He-braic idiom for a short, indefinite period of time" (Edwards, *The Gospel According to Luke*, page 406; see Hosea 6:2).

The historical record supports Jesus' pointed characterization of Jerusalem as the city that kills the prophets and stones those sent to them (Luke **13:34**; see 11:47-51). In this sense, Jesus' picture of Jew-ish people being outside of God's kingdom is not a new development. It is the continuation of a long-standing pattern of rejecting God and the ones that he has sent.

Even with Jerusalem's record of rebellion, the posture of Jesus' heart toward the city is like that of a father mourning over his son's waywardness (perhaps we are meant to see an echo of the anguish of 2 Samuel 18:33 in Jesus' repetition of "Jerusalem" in Luke **13:34**), or a hen seeking to protect her chicks. In the end, Jesus' compassion will be met with rejection; the city will neither receive Jesus nor his care or love. The reference to "your house" (**v 35**) could refer broadly to the city or perhaps more narrowly to the **temple** in particular; in either event, God's judgment will fall on them. Those who wish to be like Jesus would do well to consider his compassion for the rebellious city.

A Christian should take no delight in the condemnation of a sinner (see Ezekiel 33:11), but should be moved to tears at the thought of someone rejecting the very gospel that could save them.

> Those who wish to be like Jesus would do well to consider his compassion.

The reference to crowds calling out, "Blessed is he who comes in the name of the Lord" (Luke **13:35**) initially calls to mind Jesus' triumphal entry into the city (19:28-40), but it is unlikely that this is what Jesus is referring to for two reasons. First, Matthew places this statement after the triumphal entry (Matthew 23:39). Second, the city's rejection of Jesus in this passage does not seem to fit well with the crowd's exuberant reception of Jesus at the triumphal entry.

It is more likely that Jesus is here quoting Psalm 118:26 as a reference to his future return in judgment. At that time the people of Jerusalem will have no choice but to acknowledge Jesus as the Lord's King, the very thing they are being invited to do throughout this passage. The same is true for each of us—we will either hail Jesus as King now and so enter the great feast through the narrow door, or else we will gnash our teeth as we are forced to acknowledge him after the door has been shut.

Questions for reflection

1. How have you experienced the slow-but-inexorable nature of kingdom growth in your own life, and in the life of your church?

2. How should the width of the door into the kingdom cause us to be positive in and passionate about witnessing to others, perhaps especially those who have a generally positive view of Jesus, church, and/or their own goodness?

3. Is your natural stance toward those who reject your Lord one of compassion? If not, what emotion shapes your response instead?

3. THE PATH TO THE FEAST

"Blessed is the one who will eat at the feast in the kingdom of God" (**14:15**). But who is that one? And what road lies between today and that feast?

The image of people taking "their places at the feast in the kingdom of God" (13:29) is amplified in the parable that Jesus tells in 14:16-24. The setting is the same "house of a prominent Pharisee" where Jesus healed the man with dropsy (v 1-5), and the parable is prompted by an anonymous guest who declares to Jesus, "Blessed is the one who will eat at the feast in the kingdom of God" (**v 15**). That may strike us as slightly odd dinner-party banter, but it does make some sense in context. Again, we are being pointed to Isaiah 25:6-9, which pictured the coming of the messianic kingdom in terms of a sumptuous feast where God graciously removes the pain and disgrace of his people. And whether this guest's exclamation is motivated by genuine excitement for the arrival of God's promise or a less noble desire to impress the prominent **rabbi** with his **piety**, Jesus takes the opportunity to tell a parable that continues his ministry of pressing on his hearers their urgent need to respond properly to his call to discipleship.

Excuses, Excuses

The story that Jesus tells is fairly simple. It begins with a man giving a banquet and inviting many people (Luke **14:16**). Planning a party without the benefit of clocks and post offices and the Internet required that a servant be sent out to extend invitations and return with a sense of who would be in attendance. The planning for the feast could then proceed with the knowledge that a certain number of people had agreed to come. Once the meal was prepared, a servant was commonly dispatched to call the guests to come to table (**v 17**).

Obviously, in those days (as in ours!) to back out of the invitation at this point was very rude. But in the parable that is exactly what happens, as "they all alike began to make excuses" (**v 18**) for why they could not now attend the feast. These excuses run the range of human activity, comprising financial (**v 18**), occupational (**v 19**), and familial obligations (**v 20**). Scholars differ on whether or not these excuses are legitimate. Blomberg remarks that, "What all three share is an extraordinary lameness" (*Interpreting the Parables,* page 234). Edwards argues that if the excuses are foolish, then the sting of the parable is drawn, because "we (like the Pharisees!) may safely condemn them, and those like them" (*The Gospel According to Luke*, page 421). In the end, however, the only thing that matters is that their response has alienated and angered the host (**v 21**).

In context, it is not difficult or far-fetched to draw a straight line from the set-up of Jesus' parable to the Pharisees crowding around him at the dinner party. If, in the person of Jesus, God was extending invitations to the end-time messianic banquet, then it would seem that the strict and religious Pharisees would be at the top of the guest list. But they had responded to the invitation with a shocking rudeness and opposition (11:53-54), and so now the indignant host was prepared to act in an equally shocking way.

The host finds himself in a difficult position—a feast has been readied and the house is prepared to receive visitors, but there are no guests coming. There is no thought of canceling the banquet; instead the master sends out his servant to the small roads and back alleys of the city to bring in any guests who are willing to come: even the poor, the crippled, the blind, and the lame (**14:21**, in an echo of **v 13**). When that fails to fill the entire banquet room (**v 22**), the master extends the invitation further—even to the highways and hedges of the countryside—so that the "house will be full" (**v 23**). The opportunity to feast was now extended to the less desirable members of society—those who could not lend any prestige to the gathering and whose only qualification for attendance was their willingness to accept the invitation.

The parable continues Jesus' message that while the invitation to join God's kingdom is extended to everyone, it does require a timely response. Those fig trees that do not bear fruit during the season of the owner's patience (13:6-9) will be uprooted. Those who fail to enter through the narrow door will be excluded once it is closed (13:24-25). Those who do not come to the feast when they are called will never taste the richness of the banquet (**14:24**).

The Pharisees are clearly in the crosshairs of Jesus' teaching here, but we should not fail to see the warning for us as well. The people who "ought" to be at the party—the religious, the wealthy, the successful—are the ones who find themselves excluded. And so we are all invited to respond to Jesus' kingdom invitation, but we should not presume that our invitation is permanent. If we make other things—even good things like work and family—a priority above coming to the feast of the kingdom, we will find that we are shut out.

And if half of the parable's shock is located in the people who refuse to come to the banquet, the other half is found in those who do accept the invitation. The crippled, the poor, the blind, and the lame are not the people that we natu-

> In the kingdom, those who know they don't belong are the ones who won't miss out.

rally think of as those who have the inside track on anything, let alone God's kingdom party. But Luke's Gospel highlights the way that Jesus' arrival brings a reversal of fortune, with the poor being exalted and the powerful being brought low (see Luke 1:51-53; 6:20-26; 13:30; also 1 Corinthians 1:26-29 and James 2:5 and 5:1). In the kingdom of God, it is better to have a lowly and humble attitude than to be externally pious, rich and powerful. Those who "deserve" the invitation oftentimes do not come, but those who know that they don't belong are the ones who won't miss out on the feast. Isaac Watts' hymn "How Sweet and Aweful Is the Place" captures this sentiment perfectly:

While all our hearts and all our songs
Join to admire the feast,
Each of us cry, with thankful tongues,
"Lord, why was I a guest?"

Jesus' Guide to Table Manners

If the parable of the Great Banquet unpacks the membership of the kingdom—namely that the outsiders will find themselves inside and the insiders will find themselves outside—Jesus' other teaching at the dinner gathering illustrates how to live wisely in light of that economy. Banquets in the ancient world were oftentimes an occasion to publicly display the social status of the guests. The most important people were seated closest to the host; a seat far away from the host was an indication that you were a person of relatively little significance. At this particular gathering, it seems that the people were not assigned specific seats but were left to organize themselves. The result, as you might imagine, was a bit of posturing and jostling for the best position, with people picking "the places of honor at the table" (Luke **14:7**) for themselves. And so in this environment, Jesus tells a parable.

At first, Jesus' teaching does not seem like a parable (even though Luke refers to it as such). It strikes us perhaps more as if Jesus is giving lessons in social etiquette, how to throw a party and how to seat oneself at the table. But upon closer examination, it becomes obvious that Jesus is talking about a much larger principle: namely, the counter-intuitive nature of the kingdom of God. If you understand the meaning of the parable of the Great Banquet, with its surprise guest-list, then you will not be like those scrambling to exalt themselves at the dinner table.

In **verses 8-9**, Jesus envisions a party where a very important person shows up after the guests have been seated. At that point, the host would have to find a place of honor for them, as it would be a tremendous breach of etiquette not to give them an appropriate seat. Realistically, the host would not be willing to ask everyone at the table to shift down a spot; that would result in chaos. Instead, they will choose one person to relocate from the center of the party all the way down to the last open seat. In light of this, Jesus (with echoes of Proverbs 25:6-7) advises his audience to "take the lowest place" (Luke **14:10**) so that they will be publicly honored by their host as they are elevated to a more prominent seat. By deliberately downplaying their social status, the guest sets into motion a chain of events that will result in their receiving public honor.

As with all parables, we must be careful not to press the details too far. It is fairly safe to say that Jesus was not very concerned with making sure that his disciples received good seats at dinner parties. And he certainly is not advocating feats of **reverse psychology** to help people manipulate others into honoring them publicly to get glory in front of other people. In fact, Jesus when does get around to giving specific party-planning advice to the host in **verses 12-14**, he explicitly tells him not to plan his guest-list based on what other people can do for him.

Instead, we should understand this parable as an illustration of a principle. If you want to get ahead at a dinner party, the way forward is the opposite of what you would initially expect. In the same manner, the way to be great in the kingdom of God is to humble oneself, for God is a God who will humble those who exalt themselves, and he will exalt those who humble themselves (**v 11**—see Proverbs 3:34, which is quoted in James 4:6 and 1 Peter 5:5). It can only be this way if we are to follow a glorious King who stooped to wash his disciples' feet (John 13:1-11), the one who came not to be served but to serve (Mark 10:45) and who was exalted through the humiliation of the cross (Philippians 2:8-11).

In our day and age, we are not usually very anxious about where we are seated at a dinner party. And we may even be tempted to look down on the people in Jesus' day who were so blatantly fighting for public recognition. But we have our own ways of demonstrating favor and honor, from the number of "likes" and followers we receive on social media to the subtle way that our physical appearance and job and car and neighborhood slot us into a social pecking order. There is nothing inherently wrong with any of those things, but we run into spiritual danger when our hearts begin to crave the honor from others that attends them. The ultimate antidote to that kind of glory-hunger is finding your meaning and your honor in being the recipient of Jesus' sacrificial love. When your heart is captivated by the way that God has made much of you by sending his Son to save you, you will begin to be freed from living for the recognition of others.

> We run into spiritual danger when our hearts crave honor from others.

Those who understand the gospel of the Great Banquet ought to live with humble gratitude and generosity toward those in need. In a cruel irony, our pride is rooted both in an inflated sense of personal worth ("these people should honor me") and also in a fear that others will not share that same inflated opinion ("I will feel shame if these people do not honor me"). With its twin messages of our unworthiness to receive the invitation and God's extravagant love for us, the gospel of the Great Banquet severs both of those roots and leaves us free to find our value and worth in God's love. As Timothy Keller has written:

> "Humility is a by-product of belief in the gospel of Christ. In the gospel, we have a confidence not based in our performance but in the love of God in Christ (Romans 3:22-24). This frees us from having to always be looking at ourselves. Our sin was so great, nothing less than the death of Jesus could save us. He had to die for us. But his love for us was so great, Jesus was glad to die for us."

> ("The Advent of Humility," in *Christianity Today*, December 2008)

Questions for reflection

1. Which other priority in your life would be most likely to become an excuse for why you cannot submit to Jesus right now?

2. "Lord, why was I a guest?" How can you cultivate a humble awe that Jesus has rescued you?

3. Why is it liberating to be freed from living for the recognition of others? What difference will that make to the way you approach your work life, your life at home, your service for your church, and your thinking about evangelism?

PART TWO

Not Designed to Be Easy

We often think that our job in **evangelism** is to make being a disciple of Christ seems as easy, attractive, and painless as possible: *God has a wonderful plan for your life! You've never had a friend like Jesus! Give God a try and see if he does not come through for you!* Some evangelism strategies have more in common with the techniques of a salesperson than the ways of Jesus.

Jesus, for his part, would have made a terrible salesman. One day he was being followed by "large crowds" (Luke **14:25**), and he turned to them and said just about the least encouraging thing he could possibly say: *Do not follow me unless you hate everything you hold most dear. Yes, even your mom. And your dad. And your siblings and children. And your spouse. Even your own life* (**v 26**).

And if that were not enough to communicate the point, in **verse 27** Jesus says that being his disciple means carrying one's own cross. We have been introduced to this idea before (see 9:23), and it is hard to overstate the shock that Jesus' words would have caused. In Jesus' day, a cross was not a piece of jewelry or a symbol of love and devotion. It was a repulsive means of execution, a way of terrorizing a population and putting down dissent. The crowds in Jesus' day would have seen condemned people carrying the horizontal piece of a cross out to the place of their execution. The call to carry one's cross is a call to a one-way trip to death. That is the level of commitment that discipleship requires.

Now, Jesus' command to hate (**14:26**) might shock us, because we normally think of "hate" in terms of opposition and antipathy. But it is best to take Jesus' words here in terms of priority; Jesus must have our absolute loyalty and commitment. If love for parents or children or even one's own life threaten to interfere with that commitment, a disciple must choose to follow the will of Jesus. So, as Edwards explains,

"Hate … should not be understood in terms of emotion or malice,
but rather in its Hebraic sense, signifying the thing rejected in a
choice between two important claims."

(The Gospel According to Luke, page 426)

Count the Cost

In order to illustrate the importance of carefully considering the cost of discipleship, Jesus tells two brief parables (**v 28-30** and **v 31-32**). The ESV does a good job of reflecting the fact that each parable begins with a question that highlights the absurdity of the scenario that Jesus is proposing: "For which of you…?" (**v 28**) and "Or what king…?" (**v 31**). Both scenarios anticipate a negative answer; no one would do something like that! Jesus is inviting his hearers to see a spiritual **analogy** in a pattern of foolish behavior in the world around them.

First, imagine that you want to build a tower (**v 28**). The fact that it requires a foundation indicates that it is a significant structure, but it may well be a wise investment. Nothing in the way Jesus tells the story indicates that we should understand that this would be a foolish undertaking or a vanity project. But imagine that the builder made one crucial mistake—he began building but did not first make sure that he has the resources necessary to complete the structure. In the end, all of his labor and money would only secure for him the mockery of his neighbors (**v 29-30**) and a half-finished monument to his folly. It would have been better for him not to start the process than to quit halfway through.

In the second parable, the stakes are higher. A king who fails to gauge the relative strength of his enemy's army will suffer far more than the ridicule of his neighbors. If he commits his 10,000 troops to this battle, he will almost surely lose most of them to the 20,000 that his opponent is bringing with him (**v 31**). Does the potential reward justify the tremendous risk? Is the gain worth the price that he would have to pay? If this king decides that the cost is too steep, he will have to send out a delegation to make peace with the approaching enemy (**v 32**).

In each of the two parables, the path of wisdom is obvious. A land-owner needs to take stock to see if he can pay the price required to build a tower. A king needs be clear on whether he has what it takes to defeat an enemy. It is easy to start building a tower; it does not take much to begin a war.

But the way that Jesus starts the parable of the tower with a question in the second person ("Which of you?", ESV) forces us to put ourselves in the situation he describes: do you have the resources and commitment required to finish what you have started? The only useful tower is a completed one; if you are only going to go halfway, you might as well not begin. Like the opposing army in Jesus' parable, the call to discipleship is nothing to be trifled with or engaged with lightly. Jesus makes it clear that being his disciple will cost a person everything that they have (**v 33**). The cost of discipleship is particular to each individual. Jesus requires every person to renounce one hundred percent of what they have, whether that be very little or very much.

Does this mean that Christians cannot have personal possessions? Does following Jesus mean that we should abandon our spouses and neglect our parents and children? Of course not; that kind of flat and rigid application fails to do justice to the real point of Jesus' teaching: namely, that there can be no split loyalties in the hearts of his followers. Not everyone is called by Jesus to serve and follow him in the same way. In some ways, discipleship will look different for someone who runs a business than it will for a missionary planting churches in a remote part of the world. A mother at home with children will be called to follow Jesus in ways that are unique to her circumstance. The point is not that all give up the same things to follow Jesus, but rather, that all must be willing to give up everything they have if Jesus requires it.

In the end, there is nothing in a disciple's life that is off-limits to Jesus; following him means you have no veto powers when it comes to his plans for you. If following him requires us to give up financial security, creature comforts, good schools for our kids, the respect of others, or even our long-cherished hopes and plans for our lives, then so be it. That is the essence of what it means to hate your own life (**v 26**) and carry your cross (**v 27**).

Too often the church has tried to sell people a different, less costly form of discipleship. Preachers fill auditoriums all over the world by promising their hearers that Jesus wants nothing more than to serve them like a genie in a bottle, as if he had no other purpose than that our lives should be stuffed full of material possessions and perfect health. But what will happen when those people are confronted with Jesus' demands—that they forgo sexual immorality, that they give sacrificially, that they love unconditionally? How will those kinds of disciples not descend into bitterness when God's plan for their best life now involves a terminal cancer diagnosis? Ultimately, the false gospel of the so-called "prosperity preachers" makes false disciples; for we know that anyone who is not carrying their cross is not a true follower of Christ (**v 27**).

It is also easy for us pay lip service to the call to discipleship without actually sacrificing to follow Christ. But we should examine whether there are things that we are not willing to do, or income thresholds we are not willing to slip below, or standards of living that we could not possibly imagine forgoing, even if doing those things would advance the cause of Christ (and—let's be honest—usually they would). We should look to our lives to see if there are sinful behaviors or attitudes (maybe even things that we are able to condemn in others) that we simply will not forgo.

> There is nothing in our lives that we have the right to tell Jesus is off-limits.

There is nothing in our lives that we have the right to point to and tell Jesus that it is off-limits.

Jesus' call to radical discipleship also means that when we proclaim the gospel to unbelievers, we must tell them the whole truth.

Specifically, they must know that following Jesus means that he has a claim to everything in their lives; nothing is off-limits or outside of his lordship. If they are not told about the cost of discipleship, they may well begin down that path like the man building a tower or the king going to war, only to discover midway through that they do not have what it takes to finish the undertaking.

Will this mean that fewer people will start down the path of discipleship? Perhaps, but no fewer people will make it all the way to the end. It seems that Jesus would rather you not follow him than follow him on your terms and with your agenda. We see crowds of people as a sign of success for a church, and it may be so. But Jesus saw the crowds in **verse 25** and immediately began to clarify the parameters of discipleship so that people would follow him for the right reasons and with a proper understanding of what they would be forfeiting to do so.

There is a **paradox** at work whenever we contemplate the gospel. In a sense, the demands of the gospel will cost us everything in our lives; some of those things may be good (such as money or personal comfort) and some may be bad (such as selfishness and sin). But in the end, the message of the gospel is that we receive far more from the Lord Jesus than we could ever possibly sacrifice. All of the comfort, health, and pleasure of this world is rubbish compared to the forgiveness, love, **adoption**, and eternal life that we receive when we are in Christ (see Philippians 3:7-11). The pleasures of sin cannot compare with the reward that God has promised to his people (see Hebrews 11:24-27). In that light, we should remember that the call to radical discipleship in Luke **14:26-33** is ultimately good news. It is a call to trade in those things that we cannot possibly keep and that cannot ultimately satisfy us for a far greater inheritance that we cannot possibly lose.

The question that each person must wrestle with is: Does Jesus seem worth it to you? A Christian is not a glutton for punishment, someone who takes a perverse joy in pain and difficulty. Instead, a

Christian is someone who understands the sacrifice, but who believes that the sacrifice is worth the rewards that come with following Jesus. If we do not enter into discipleship with our eyes wide open, knowing the costs but prizing the benefits more, then we will give up somewhere along the way. We will be like the man who built half a tower before realizing that he did not have enough to finish.

Salty Followers

Luke concludes this section about discipleship with a warning. Salt is good, but if it loses its saltiness it cannot be useful for anything (**v 34-35**). The meaning of Jesus' word picture is debated, and Edwards compiles four different theories about how salt might lose its saltiness (*The Gospel According to Luke*, page 430, note 61):

- It might be compromised by the presence of other compounds.

- It might be used for "catalytic purposes in ovens" and thus undergo a chemical change.

- It could lose its impact when mixed with too many or the wrong kind of spices.

- Or, Jesus knows that salt does not lose its saltiness, and therefore the saying suggests that the scenario Jesus is referring to is impossible.

If the fourth suggestion is correct (and it seems to fit best with the context), then the thrust of Jesus' teaching is that a half-hearted disciple is no disciple at all; it is impossible for a disciple to be anything less than a devoted follower of Christ. Though all followers of Christ will struggle with indwelling sin that makes the intensity of our devotion less than it should be, our desire and intention is to follow Jesus without reservations. Anything less than that posture of the heart is useless discipleship. We might find that message a bit strident or extreme, but Luke concludes this section of his Gospel with a ringing warning: "Whoever has ears to hear, let them hear" (**v 35**).

Questions for reflection

1. "Jesus requires every person to renounce one hundred percent of what they have, whether that be very little or very much." Does that describe you? Why / why not?

2. When are you most tempted to adopt a "salesman mentality" to the demands of discipleship—either in conversation with other believers, with non-Christians, or with yourself?

3. In what area of your life are you most likely to ignore Jesus' teaching here, instead of having ears to hear?

4. SHEEP, COINS, AND SONS

What kind of person does God love?

How do you begin to answer that kind of question? In our thera-peutic "self-esteem" culture, the default assumption of most people seems to be that God loves everybody. We have been taught to accept ourselves the way that we are, to embrace our faults and let go of any negative thoughts that we might have about ourselves and the things that we have done. Surely, if God is love (1 John 4:8), then he must love everyone equally.

But that does not seem to do justice to the world that we live in. It seems that virtually everyone could agree that God must disapprove of some kinds of people. Hitler, Pol Pot and Stalin all come to mind. Whatever personal conception of God someone might hold, it prob-ably involves him disapproving of genocide and torture. And most of us would include terrorists and other kinds of more run-of-the-mill murderers on that list. We can probably agree that we do not want God to love and accept those kinds of people.

But what if we get a little closer to home. How should God feel about unfaithful husbands? How does he view mothers who lose their temper and hit their children? Does he love alcoholics, lazy employees, people who cheat on their taxes, and people with anger issues? What about people that are proud, or people who use hurtful words, or people who are selfish?

The answer to these kinds of questions gets right to the heart of who God is and how people relate to him. And the three parables that Luke records in chapter 15 go a long way toward providing Jesus' answer to the question: What kind of person does God love?

Context

Luke tips us off that the parables that comprise chapter 15 need to be understood in terms of the setting in which they were told. We are accustomed to Jesus spending time with the scandalously unworthy (**15:1**; see 5:29-32; 7:34). The muttering disapproval of the religious leaders (**15:2**; compare Exodus 16:2, 7-8) seems to be based in more than the mere fact that Jesus was tolerating the fact that "the tax collectors and sinners were all gathering around to hear" him (Luke **15:1**), though that was certainly objectionable enough. Far worse to their minds was the fact that he was actively cultivating fellowship with these kinds of people; he was actually welcoming and eating with them.

It is interesting that the same Jesus who stressed the radical obedience required by discipleship (14:25-35) is the one who also pursued relationships with notorious sinners. But it seems that Jesus knew that the crowds of would-be followers (14:25) needed to have their enthusiasm tempered lest they enter into discipleship without counting the cost. On the other hand, the Pharisees and teachers of the law needed just the opposite lesson. Their pride and presumption needed to be confronted with the reality of God's special mercy and love for the lost. The teaching that follows serves as both an explanation and a correction.

The One Lost Sheep

By telling them his first parable (**15:3**), Jesus draws his hearers into a difficult dilemma by encouraging them to "suppose one of you has a hundred sheep and loses one of them" (**v 4**). We are not told how the sheep was lost, but presumably either it wandered away from the flock on its own or was carried off by a predator. But whatever the cause, on the face of it the mathematics work against that missing sheep. The risks of heading out to look for it are significant; if it had wandered into the wilderness, the terrain would be treacherous and dangers would be plentiful.

Upon careful reflection, it hardly seems to make practical sense to leave the ninety-nine sheep vulnerable and unprotected on the un-likely chance that one wandering sheep can be located. Could that one missing sheep be valuable enough in the eyes of the shepherd that he would contemplate leaving the ninety-nine behind in order to search for it? Despite all of the reasons why the shepherd might decide to simply write off the wandering sheep, Jesus' assumption is that his hearers will agree on what he would do: "Doesn't he leave the ninety-nine in the open country and go after the lost sheep until he finds it?" (**v 4**). The one lost sheep receives all of the attention and care of its master.

This little vignette has a happy ending! The conclusion to the story is all about joy—the shepherd finds his missing lamb and carries it home on his shoulders "joyfully" (**v 5**). So great is his delight over the safe return of the one sheep that he calls together his friends and neighbors, urging them to rejoice with him (**v 6**). In the end, his re-sponse cannot be understood in purely economic terms; he may well spend more than the value of the sheep celebrating its return with his friends. Jesus' hearers are left contemplating the shepherd's extraordi-nary love for this one lost sheep.

How to Find a Lost Coin

The second parable serves as a parallel to the first (a **literary device** to which we have grown accustomed—see 13:18-21 and 14:28-32). The story in this case invites us to consider a woman who has lost one of her ten silver coins (**15:8**). The Greek text indicates that the coin is a drachma, roughly the equivalent of a day's wage for a typical laborer; certainly a normal person would be anxious to recover such a sum as quickly as possible. As with so many of Jesus' parables, we are quickly engaged personally in the action. Who has not had the experience of looking for a lost earring, set of car keys or computer file? That specific mix of frustration, anticipation, and dread is familiar to everyone, and so is her course of action. Jesus asks rhetorically, "Doesn't she light a lamp, sweep the house and search carefully until she finds it?" (**v 8**).

If this woman is of modest means, her floor may not have been paved with stones and she may not have had windows to let in light. Locating a coin in the dark on an uneven earth floor would not be a simple task. For that reason, she would have to light a lamp, sweep the floor, and conduct a thorough search until the lost item has been located. If her efforts mirror that of the shepherd (**v 4**), so does her response to finding what she had lost. After her careful search meets with success, she too calls together her "friends and neighbors" to share in her joy (**v 9**).

The Lost and the Loved

It is not difficult to discern where these two parables intersect with the situation in which Jesus told them; Jesus is offering an explanation for and defense of his behavior. The Pharisees and teachers of the law were scandalized by his decision to pursue fellowship with tax collectors and sinners. Jesus, for his part, casts his love for those far from God in terms of the love and delight that we all take in finding things that we have lost. If we can easily relate to the delight we might take in finding something like a lost coin or sheep, how much more would we expect that God (here referred to **obliquely** by the word "heaven") would rejoice when a human being who is lost in their sins repents and comes home (**v 7, 10**)? The point is that God loves lost people in just the same way that a shepherd loves a lost sheep and this woman loves her lost coin.

Jesus is confronting the religious leaders with their failure to understand what brings joy to God. They believe that God delights in those people who, like themselves, seem righteous. But Jesus has already made it clear that there is no one who is so righteous that they do not need to repent (13:5). The need for repentance is universal, for we have all gone astray like sheep (Isaiah 53:6), and so we should resist the temptation to read too much into Jesus' description of the ninety-nine righteous people who have no need of repentance in Luke **15:7** (we have seen a similar expression in 5:31-32).

In fact, in this interaction, the irony is that the people who are most truly lost are those who identify themselves with the ninety-nine "good" sheep that do not need to be found. The Pharisees' perception of their own righteousness means that they cannot hear Jesus' call to repentance as a call to them. Because they are not lost in obvious and spectacular ways (like the tax collectors and sinners), they miss out on the fact that they also need to be found. The good news of God's love is not that he loves the "righteous," for there are no such people. The good news is that he is merciful; his forgiving and restoring love extends to every single person who repents.

The two little stories that Jesus tells are so vivid and engaging that it is easy to miss the larger point. Neither the lost sheep nor the lost coin is the main character in the parable; the center of each story is the passionate search that is undertaken in order to find the lost item. What is the love of God like? It is like a shepherd who would go to extremes (leaving his flock, traveling all over the wilderness, and carrying a hundred-pound animal on his shoulders) in order to see his lost sheep restored. The love of God is like the sick-to-her-stomach sensation a woman would feel if she discovers that 10% of her personal wealth has gone missing; nothing will be right until the coin is found. For such a woman, no effort will be spared in order to retrieve the lost item.

> Jesus is the divine rescue mission; he is the heavenly search party.

That explains the ministry of Jesus. He is the divine rescue mission; he is the heavenly search party. He came to return sinners to fellowship with God by his death on the cross and resurrection from the grave. Just as the shepherd and the woman spared no effort in order to experience the joy of finding what had been lost, so Jesus endured the pain and humiliation of the cross for the joy of seeing lost people restored to God (Hebrews 12:2). Just as the sheep contributed nothing to their rescue except for getting themselves lost in the first place, so our only hope of being saved is if God himself does 100% of the job. Your lostness is all you contribute to your salvation.

What kind of person does God love? Jesus' answer would have shocked the Pharisees, and it may shock us as well. It turns out that God does not delight in those who seem to be righteous; he is not passionate about rewarding those who feel they deserve his favor by their performance. His love is not reserved for good, decent, law-abiding people. Instead, he loves those who are lost. He delights when they are restored to fellowship with him.

Can you understand why this is good news? If God's love followed the Pharisees' program, then we would all be lost. None of us are righteous enough to deserve God's love. And even if we were, that would mean that we would always be in danger of doing something wrong and forfeiting divine favor. But thankfully, God's love is always rooted in his own character, and never finally in our goodness and obedience.

If you struggle to believe that God loves you, then consider the thrust of these parables. If you have turned to Christ through repentance and faith, then God delights in you. He takes joy in your return to him, not because you are so holy and righteous nor because you never mess up. God takes costly, party-throwing joy in you because, in the end… it brings him delight to love you.

Questions for reflection

1. How does it make you feel to reflect on the truth that God sought you out to rescue you?

2. How does it make you feel that when you first repented, heaven resounded to sounds of joy?

3. What will it look like for your passion and your joy to be aligned with God's?

PART TWO

The next parable (15:11-32) is one of Jesus' best-known and best-loved parables. While it is much longer than the two that precede it, it addresses the same situation and amplifies the same principles. **Verses 11-12** introduce us to three characters: a man and his two sons. Over the course of the parable, each of the three individuals behaves in striking ways that teach something important about the dynamic described in verses 1-2. They are worthy of being considered individually.

The Younger Son

The story begins with the younger son asking his father for his share of his inheritance (**v 12**). In that culture the older son could expect to inherit two thirds of his father's estate; the younger son could anticipate receiving the rest. But what is irregular in the request is not the amount that he asks for (he simply requests "my share"), but the fact that he wants it before his father has died. In essence, he is communicating that he wants to break all ties and associations with the family. He is planning to leave home and does not anticipate any further contact with his father, so he had better take his inheritance with him now. He wants to start relating to his father now the way that he will once his father is dead; to put it bluntly, he wants to skip ahead to the point where he can have his father's money without having his father.

We are not told why the young man felt this way. Perhaps he felt that his father was too strict. Maybe he felt penned in and unable to express himself at home. Maybe he was simply selfish and ungrateful. Whatever the cause, there is a seemingly irreparable breach in the relationship when the father grants the son's request and divides his property between his children (**v 12**). The younger son surely leaves home anticipating the life of unbridled fun and pleasure that is available to a young man with a lot of money in his pocket: friends, food, drink, and women.

The fun does not last for long, though. The "wild living," as Jesus delicately puts it in **verse 13**, quickly drains the young man's financial resources. When a severe famine hits the region (**v 14**), he finds himself without any money, friends, or prospects. In the end, his only option is to take a job feeding pigs (**v 15**) in order to survive.

The picture here is of a young man who has lost everything. He has no family and no money. In a **Gentile** country (for nowhere else would we find a pig farmer—no Jew would ever keep pigs!), he has lost even his cultural and religious identity. The word that Luke uses in **verse 15** (*exollethe*—translated by the NIV as "hired himself") has the sense of binding or gluing something. He has become identified with the citizens of "that country," outside the bounds of Jewish identity and reduced to longing to eat the pods that pigs eat (**v 16**) but not even receiving that much. It is safe to say that a person could not fall much lower.

The man's desperation grants him a healthy measure of clarity, however. Many Christians can look back to a time when God in his kindness made them miserable enough in their sin that they finally called out to him for help (see Hebrews 12:7-11). "Coming to himself" (the literal translation of Luke **15:17**), he realized the mistake that he had made. Perhaps he had been wrong about his father all along; life on the farm was not so bad. After all, even his father's hired servants had more bread than they needed! He realized that life with his father was a life of real blessing, and that it was better than life pursuing happiness out in the world.

The plan that he hatches is a mixture of audacity and humility. He will approach his father, admit his fault (**v 18**), and beg for some small kind of restoration. It is certainly too much to ask to be accepted back into the family as a son, but perhaps the sight of his emaciated child will move the father to compassion and he could be treated like a hired servant (**v 19**). So the younger son gets up and returns home (**v 20**).

It is not too hard to see that the character of the younger son helps to explain the experience of the people who had been flocking to Jesus.

Like the young man, the tax collectors and sinners had wandered far from "home" in their rebellion against God and his law. But just as he had come to his senses and humbled himself, so they were repentantly seeking to be restored to their heavenly father through Jesus. In this way we are engaged with the main tension of the parable: how will the father react? It is all well and good for the young man to decide to head home, but it is all for nothing if his father will not take him back. In the same way sinners can repent all they want, but the only question that matters is whether the heavenly Father is disposed to receive repentant sinners into his family.

The Father

We can imagine that the younger son's heart was pounding as he neared the family estate, rehearsing over and over his plea for mercy. But what he found was that his father, seeing him from a long way off (was he watching for him?), was "filled with compassion for him" (**v 20**). There was no suspense or ambiguity in the reception, for in his joy the father broke with all decorum and ran to meet his son, throwing his arms around him and kissing him.

The son begins humbly to unfold his request for restoration to a place of service in the household (**v 21**), but he can only begin to acknowledge his sin before the father interrupts him with a lavish welcome. There is no question of him being treated like a hired hand or having to endure a probation period; the father orders his servants to quickly bring a robe, ring, and sandals for his son (**v 22**). As Edwards points out, all three are signs of "status, reputation, and honor" (*The Gospel According to Luke*, page 176). The killing of a calf was an extreme extravagance (**v 23**), but this was a once-in-a-lifetime celebration—the son who was dead in his estrangement and rebellion has been restored to life (**v 24**).

If you are familiar with this story, it can be hard to appreciate how unexpected this response is. The younger son's behavior was truly scandalous. The father could not have been blamed if he had responded to his son's return with suspicion and distance, but instead his love was lavish and unrestrained. There was no question of the young man returning as a servant, for he was a son!

The great Victorian preacher Charles H. Spurgeon reflected on the picture of God's love for the lost in this parable in his sermon "Many Kisses For Returning Sinners" (accessible at time of publication at spurgeon.org/sermons/2236.php):

> "The condescension of God towards penitent sinners is very great. He seems to stoop from His throne of glory to fall upon the neck of a repentant sinner. God on the neck of a sinner! What a wonderful picture! Can you conceive it? I do not think you can; but if you cannot imagine it, I hope that you will realize it. When God's arm is about our neck, and His lips are on our cheek, kissing us much, then we understand more than preachers or books can ever tell us of His condescending love."

This parable is Jesus' way of putting a fine point on the lesson of the previous two parables—if we rejoice in the restoration of relatively unimportant things like sheep and coins, how much more does God rejoice when human beings that are made in his own image are returned to him through repentance?

The Older Brother

We are introduced to the older brother in **verse 25**, where we find him dutifully working out in the fields. The contrast between the two sons could not be starker: while the one left the family to squander his money in shameful ways, the other stayed and served his father obediently (**v 29**). He had appeared a model son; but when he finds out the reason for the celebration going on in the house (**v 26-27**), he can barely be civil, such is his anger (**v 28**). His bitterness pours out as he describes his time working for his father as "slaving" (**v 29**), and as he then tries to pour cold water on the father's joy by reminding him that "this son of yours" (not "this brother of mine"!) squandered the family fortune on prostitutes (**v 30**).

Viewed from a certain angle, his outraged reaction is perfectly understandable. After all, the father's celebration is a bit like a slap in his face. It hardly seems fair that his diligence and loyalty have never been rewarded with even a small party and a young goat to eat. But here his brother acts in the most irresponsible way imaginable and his father rolls out the red carpet! How is he expected to be pleased with that?

It is clear that the older brother is meant to show the Pharisees how their muttering about Jesus' ministry places them outside of God's program of restoration and forgiveness. They saw Jesus proclaiming that the tax collectors and sinners could "come home" to God and receive the warmest welcome, and instead of rejoicing in the goodness of God's mercy, they complained about the unfairness of it all. The parable ends with a surprising reversal of fortune— the younger brother is inside the house celebrating his relationship with his father, but the older brother is on the outside, suddenly estranged from his father.

The Invitation

The father's love for his lost younger son is matched by his patience for his suddenly lost older son. We could well imagine that he might have berated the young man for his ingratitude and selfishness. After all, who is the son to tell his father what to do with his time and money? But instead the father pleads with him, reminding him that his service has not been in vain (**v 31**). The parable ends in with an implicit plea for the older brother to come in, rejoice in his father's kindness to the lost brother, and join the party (**v 32**). We are left hanging with the question, *Will the older brother come in?*

These three parables extend an invitation to everyone. Some people, like the younger brother and the tax collectors and sinners, have looked to find life in riotous living. Instead of rejoicing in God they have wandered away, imagining that the pleasures of sin make life ultimately satisfying. Jesus called (and still calls) these kinds people to come to their senses and repent. If they will, they can be sure of a warm welcome from their heavenly Father.

But people who believe that their obedience to God means that they (and only they!) should be rewarded by God—people like many of the Pharisees—are just as lost as the most hardened sinner. In fact, their case may be worse, because they are blinded to their need for repentance. Their lives look more put together and so it is harder for them to get to a place where they "come to their senses" (see what it took to get the attention of the Pharisee named Saul—Acts 9:1-19). The fact that the parable of the Prodigal Son ends with a cliff-hanger (will the older brother join his father's party?) puts the spotlight squarely on the Pharisees—will they drop their attempts to earn God's blessing by their performance and join the salvation that Jesus is bringing?

These three parables are about the incredible truth that God loves sinners with a joyous, passionate love. If the Pharisees and teachers of the law had really known and loved God, they would have been out calling sinners to repentance like Jesus was. They should have known better, for back in the book of Ezekiel, God had complained about the leaders of his people using language that is strikingly familiar to Jesus' imagery in Luke 15:

"Should not shepherds take care of the flock? You eat the curds, clothe yourselves with the wool and slaughter the choice animals, but you do not take care of the flock. You have not strengthened the weak or healed the sick or bound up the injured. You have not brought back the strays or searched for the lost. You have ruled them harshly and brutally. So they were scattered because there was no shepherd, and when they were scattered they became food for all the wild animals. My sheep wandered over all the mountains and on every high hill. They were scattered over the whole earth, and no one searched or looked for them."

(Ezekiel 34:2-6)

But in his love, God had a plan to find his lost sheep. In fact he would do the work himself:

> "For this is what the Sovereign LORD says: I myself will search for my sheep and look after them. As a shepherd looks after his scattered flock when he is with them, so will I look after my sheep. I will rescue them from all the places where they were scattered on a day of clouds and darkness. I will bring them out from the nations and gather them from the countries, and I will bring them into their own land. I will pasture them on the mountains of Israel, in the ravines and in all the settlements in the land." (v 11-13)

Jesus represents the ultimate fulfillment of that promise. He is the good shepherd who pursues the sheep. He does what the older brother in the parable should have done: he pursues the lost children of his Father.

> The question is whether we love the same things that our heavenly Father does.

The question for us is whether we love the same things that our heavenly Father loves. Followers of Jesus should be marked by a compassionate tenderness toward people who are in rebellion against God. We should actively pursue them, working as deputy shepherds seeking to bring lost sheep back to the fold. And when a sinner repents and "comes home" through faith in Christ, we ought to be filled with delight that our God is a merciful Father who forgives and restores the lost. Rightly did James Montgomery Boice write:

> "We are never so like God as when we rejoice at the salvation of sinners. We are never so like Satan as when we despise those are thus converted and think ourselves superior to them."
>
> (*The Parables of Jesus,* page 56)

Questions for reflection

1. Do you know anyone who is living as the younger son in the distant country right now? What will you pray? What might you do?

2. Are you in any danger of living as the older son at the end of the story right now? Do you need to stop parading your goodness and demanding blessing from God, and simply enjoy his presence?

3. How have these three parables caused you to love Jesus more?

5. SPENDING DECISIONS

If Luke 15 contains some of Jesus' most famous and accessible parables, chapter 16 contains some of the most obscure and confusing. The so-called Parable of the Shrewd Tenant is not a confusing story, per se, but some of the application that Jesus makes can seem puzzling.

Dishonesty Commended?

In **verse 1**, the disciples are introduced to "a rich man whose manager was accused of wasting his possessions" (the word translated as "wasting" is the same used in 15:13 to describe the younger son's squandering of his wealth). A manager was typically a servant who was responsible for overseeing the operation of the entire household, and so it was imperative to have a person who was both competent and trustworthy in that position. We are not told what this particular manager has done to occasion reports of mismanagement, but there must be some truth to the accusations, for when he is confronted by his master in **16:2** he does not bother to defend himself.

Instead, he hatches a scheme. He knows both that he cannot retain his current position and also that some options (manual labor and begging) are not suitable for him (**v 3**). So he comes up with a plan that will ensure that people will welcome him into their homes once he has lost his employment (**v 4**). His scheme begins with calling in each of his master's debtors and asking them how much they owe him (**v 5**). Most likely, these are well-off businessmen who have contracted to farm the master's land, in return for which they owe him a portion of the produce. The manager most likely asks them to declare the amount of their debt, not because he is unaware of the amount, but because he wants them to be accomplices to the deceit he is about to unfold. Because of their complicity, they will be much more likely to help him in his time of need.

The first debtor owes nine hundred gallons (3,000 liters) of oil (**v 6**—literally "a hundred baths of oil"): roughly the yearly amount that would be produced by 150 olive trees or three years of wages for a normal laborer. Since he has not yet lost his employment, the manager still has the authority to negotiate agreements with his master's clients. And so he offers the man a deal that is too good to pass up—he will approve a new note for half of the original amount.

The second debtor owes a thousand bushels (30 tons) of wheat (**v 7**—literally "a hundred kors of wheat"). That represents the yearly yield of a hundred acres, or almost a decade's worth of wages for a laborer. That extraordinary sum may explain why this man receives a relatively smaller discount (20% as opposed to the 50% the other man is given). Both debtors, through no effort of their own, receive a discount worth about 1.5 to 2 years' worth of salary for an average worker. We can assume that the manager continues this pattern with all of the master's debtors, thus ingratiating himself with a large group of people who now might feel obligated to extend hospitality toward him in his time of need.

By virtue of this stunt, it seems that the manager "fails every test in the dispatch of his office" (Edwards, *The Gospel According to Luke*, page 452). As a result, we might well expect that the master would greet the servant's scheme with anger and perhaps even some form at retribution. After all, this stunt has costs him somewhere in the neighborhood of $100,000. But when the matter is discovered, "the master commended the dishonest manager because he had acted shrewdly" (**v 8**). This conclusion is a total shock; why would the master praise his servant for being unrighteous and dishonest? Potential explanations for the master's reaction abound, including:

- The reduction of the debts makes the master look generous and enhances his honor in the eyes of his debtors. This is unlikely, however, because the manager's furtive manner (he tells them to forge new documents "quickly" in **verse 6**) would communicate clearly to the debtors that he is acting without the approval of his employer.

- The master must pretend to have authorized the scheme; otherwise he will be shamed by his lack of control over his household. This is possible, but it seems that **verses 1-2** indicate that the master's problems with this servant are already public knowledge.

- The reduction of each debt is in reality just expunging the amount of interest that the master is charging the debtors in violation of the Law of Moses (Deuteronomy 23:19). Thus, the manager's dishonesty is actually a way of bringing the business into compliance with God's will. This is technically possible, but it is hard to imagine the master charging 100% interest on his loans, especially in light of the law's prohibition.

- The amount by which each debt is reduced is really the manager's personal commission, meaning that he is only giving away his own money. This is also unlikely, for such astronomical sums seem like an excessive commission for a servant, and this will not explain either why the servant acts secretly or why his behavior is labeled as (literally) "unrighteous" in Luke **16:8**.

In the end, we are probably best simply to be content with Jesus' explanation for the master's positive reaction, "For the people of this world are more shrewd in dealing with their own kind than are the people of the light" (**v 8**). The master's approval is not a reward for dishonesty, but a tip of the hat to the servant's shrewdness. In terms of sheer self-preservation, this scoundrel cannot be outfoxed; he has gone to great lengths to secure his own interests. The master could choose to be angry about the development, but he cannot do anything about it at this point, so he might as well admire the man's shrewdness.

Shrewd Disciples?

Some Christians have struggled with this parable because it seems that Jesus is commending dishonesty and theft in the service of self-interest. But we would do well to remember that interpreting the parables often requires us to separate out one or two main points while leaving behind some of the details of the story. The very nature of telling a story in order to make a point means that some things in the story are not literally true or are not relevant on their own. There are details that are subordinate to the bigger point.

For example, we should not conclude from the so-called Parable of the Great Banquet (Luke 14:15-24) that God is taken off guard when people refuse his invitation, or that the offer of a place at his end-time feast is only offered to lowly people as an afterthought. As we have seen, the specific lesson that Jesus is teaching relates to the way that the Pharisees respond to God (or fail to), and the way that they view those who do respond to God. This is why Jesus can use images like an unjust judge or a thief in the night to make a point about how God will act. He's not saying that everything that is true about that person in the parable is true of God. Instead, he's trying to show how one aspect of the behavior of the judge or thief is **analogous** to God's actions. In the same way, we are safe to conclude that Jesus is not commending dishonesty to his disciples. Instead, he is commending to us a specific aspect of the manager's actions (his shrewdness) without condoning or encouraging all of the other things the manager does.

At the end of **16:8**, Jesus drives home his point: the people who belong to the world and all its values (literally "the sons of this age") know how to get what they want from other people through clever planning and activity. God's children (literally "the sons of light"), however, sometimes fail to see how they can shrewdly use the things of this world to their spiritual advantage. The citizens of the world know how to take care of their needs and make sure they get what they want. The dishonest steward behaves wisely according to the world's standards and the world's values. In an analogous way, Jesus wants his followers to behave wisely according to the standards and values of his kingdom. We are to be kingdom-shrewd with everything at our disposal.

> Jesus wants us to be kingdom-shrewd with everything at our disposal.

Jesus applies this principle specifically to the way that his followers use their "worldly wealth" (a phrase that is found in both **verse 9** and **verse 11**—literally "**mammon** of unrighteousness"). That phrase does not indicate wealth that is obtained through illicit means, for Jesus assumes that his followers will have worldly wealth in their possession. Instead, we should understand that Jesus is referring to the kind of wealth that belongs to this unrighteous world. He is not talking about treasures in heaven (12:33), but the cash and coins that drive so much of daily life here on earth.

Because that kind of wealth will fail you (**16:9**—notice that it is a matter of "when" it will be gone, not "if" it will be gone), Jesus urges his disciples to use it shrewdly while it lasts. Whether through natural disaster, theft, market fluctuations, or simply the expiration of our life here on earth, there will come a time when our wealth will disappear. Like the manager in the parable, you are coming up on a day where this current state of affairs will be over. The question is whether you will use the resources at hand (whatever worldly wealth you might have) to prepare yourself for the future. Jesus wants you to act shrewdly now in order to secure your own best interests on that future day. Use the money now to prepare yourself for the future.

Jesus' specific instruction is to use this wealth to "gain friends for yourselves." That is to say, we should live with the kind of generosity that is attractive to others; after all, generous people usually have lots of friends. One of the blessings of these friendships is that when your money fails you, you will be welcomed "into eternal dwellings."

Who are the ones doing the welcoming in **verse 9**? Three options are possible :

- ■ The "they" represents the friends one made on earth. If they precede us to heaven, they will welcome us there when we arrive.

- ■ The "they" represents God's angels, who welcome us into heaven on behalf of God.

- ■ The "they" is an oblique way of referring to God, who rewards the one whose love for him moves him to generosity.

Whichever referent is correct (and the first is the most natural way to read the parable), the point is the same: be generous now so as to accrue benefit for yourself in heaven. Who knows how our acts of service, our faithful sharing of the gospel, and our generosity might impact other people's lives and result in a warm welcome in heaven?

Investment Advice

Luke rounds out the themes of the parable with some of Jesus' other teachings about money. The larger point of these teachings is that the way we handle our worldly wealth (such wealth being something of relatively little eternal importance) is a matter of eternal significance. The person who is honest with a little will be honest with much (**v 10**), but if we can't be trusted to handle "worldly wealth," God will not trust us with true (that is, heavenly) riches (**v 11**). We, like the manager in the parable, are stewards of another's wealth. All of our money is from God; we are to use it in a "trustworthy" manner (**v 12**) or else we should not expect "property of [our] own" in the life to come (see 1 Corinthians 6:2 and 2 Corinthians 5:10).

In the end, our relationship to money is one of love and service. Because money is so powerful and seductive, we are easily tempted to give our whole lives in service to it. Money can purchase access to the best food and medicine, it can insulate us from the vagaries of the market, and it can open the door to the most exciting experiences. It gives us a measure of safety, security, and happiness that can seem much more tangible and immediate than God's provision of all of those things for his people. For those reasons, money makes a powerful competitor to God's claim on our hearts and lives.

The miser, the workaholic, the over-spender, and the person who spends a great portion of their time worrying about their finances each lives in service to unrighteous wealth. The Pharisees fell into this category (Luke **16:14**), and so they could do nothing but sneer at Jesus' teaching. Their service to the master of mammon meant there was no room in their lives for them to serve God. Their hearts were committed to one master (money), and so without realizing it, they had grown to despise the other (God—**v 13**).

Our finances represent one important arena in which our discipleship is played out; our bank statement will reveal the things that we truly love. We can pay lip service to generosity toward the things of God, but the One who sees our hearts (**v 15**) knows perfectly well whether we love him or our money. That is why we do not interpret these teachings in a mercenary way, as if Jesus is telling us that we can buy God's approval by cutting a check to the church each month. No, God is after our hearts and our love. He wants followers whose hearts have been made generous by the incredible generosity that God has shown to them (see Romans 8:32).

Questions for reflection

1. "Our bank statement will reveal the things that we truly love." What does yours reveal? To what extent are you kingdom-shrewd with your finances?

2. Western culture is a materialistic culture. What blindspots do you think this causes in your life and church when it comes to spending your money with kingdom priorities?

3. In what ways is Jesus a better God to serve than Money? Why is this easy to forget in day-to-day life?

PART TWO

The end of the previous section has begun to shift the focus of Jesus' teaching from his disciples (Luke 16:1) to the Pharisees, those lovers of money (**v 14**). They objected to everything about Jesus' ministry, from his teaching about money in the previous passage to his friendship with sinners and tax collectors (see 15:1-2). Jesus confounded them by his approach to the Scriptures; on one hand he seemed utterly unconcerned to keep their rules (see 13:14-15 and 14:1-6), but on the other he seemed to press for an even higher standard of obedience and righteousness for his followers (see Matthew 5:20). In Luke **16:16-18**, Jesus seeks to explain to the Pharisees the ways in which his ministry is both a break from the Old Testament era and also a continuation of it.

Discontinuity and Continuity

In **verse 16**, Jesus says that the Law and the Prophets (shorthand for the Old Testament Scriptures) were proclaimed until John. John the Baptist was the last messenger of the old covenant era. Now that Jesus had arrived, things were going to be different. The Law and the Prophets described a certain time and place and way of behaving toward God, but they also saw a day coming where there would be a new covenant and things would change fundamentally (see Jeremiah 31:31-34). The arrival of the Messiah represented the beginning of that new era, and so the old way of doing things became defunct. Now the good news of the kingdom is being preached and the promise of the Law and the Prophets has been fulfilled. We no longer relate to God as Old Testament believers did, through faith in an as-yet-unfulfilled promise, but we relate to him based on faith in what he did for us through the death and resurrection of his Son.

Now, Jesus says, everyone is forcing his or her way into this kingdom (Luke **16:16**). The phrase can be understood in a number of ways, but in context the most likely sense is that people are now strenuously urged to enter God's kingdom. The arrival of the fulfillment of the promise means that people come to God through faith in Christ, and not through the Old Testament law.

Should we understand that Jesus came to undermine or dismantle the ministry of the Old Testament? Jesus warns against that misunderstanding in **verse 17**, saying that though the Old Testament has been supplanted by the proclamation of the good news of the kingdom, "the least stroke of a pen" can never "drop out of the Law." Instead, Jesus understood that his arrival signified the fulfillment of the law (see Matthew 5:17-18). Far from nullifying the law, Jesus was bringing it to its ultimate purpose. He was fulfilling the promise and meaning of the Old Testament in his life, his teaching, and his substitutionary death and resurrection.

Free From the Law?

The natural question then is whether the follower of Christ is free from the moral obligations of the law. The Pharisees, of course, would be very quick to spot and criticize any suggestion from Jesus that he was relaxing God's moral strictness. But while the Old Testament law is no longer binding on the believer (with its dietary restrictions and sacrificial system), the good news of the kingdom does not mean that God no longer cares about the holiness of his people. In fact, just the opposite is true.

Jesus makes that point in Luke **16:18**, where he presents a moral obligation for his people: specifically that they should not pursue divorce in order to marry someone else. To do so, even though it might technically be within the bounds of the Old Testament law, would amount to adultery, for it represents a fundamental unfaithfulness to the original marriage vows. While there are cases where divorce and remarriage are permissible, such as where there is unfaithfulness (Matthew 19:9) or abandonment (1 Corinthians 7:15), the general principle stands: remarriage after a divorce is normally forbidden.

Jesus' words here represent a more rigorous **ethical** standard than that which is contained in the Old Testament. The law contained regulations for how divorce should be handled so that the woman, who was the more vulnerable party in the proceedings, would not be destroyed in the process. But here Jesus presses on his followers the expectation that they will seek to go beyond the law and comply with God's original intent for marriage. The arrival of the kingdom does not nullify the law, but transforms the hearts of its citizens so that they will long to obey God's will (see Jeremiah 31:33).

The Parable of the Rich Man and Lazarus

Initially, the parable in Luke 16:19-31 seems to have little connection to what comes before it. But the phrase "there was a rich man" (**v 19**) parallels the introduction of the previous parable (v 1) and the unexpected introduction of Moses and the prophets into the story (**v 29-31**) indicates that we are meant to understand this story in the larger context of the chapter.

Jesus, the master storyteller, introduces a series of contrasts between the two main characters that sets the scene in a quick and dramatic fashion. The first man was rich. He enjoyed all the luxuries that worldly wealth could provide (**v 19**). The second man, Lazarus, was a poor beggar (**v 20**). He was laid (literally "was thrown") outside the rich man's gate where he could beg for food and money. His life was one of suffering and longing—the fact that he "was laid" outside the gate and was unable to protect himself from the indignity of having his sores licked by wild, disease-ridden dogs (**v 21**) seems to indicate that he was in some way an invalid.

In a world with no organized social-relief programs, people in Lazarus' position were dependent on the generosity of people like the rich man (a generosity on which the Old Testament law insisted—see Deuteronomy 15:7-8 for one example). The rich man was clearly aware of Lazarus' presence at his gate and his extreme need, for he knew the beggar's name without being told (Luke **16:24**). But there is no indication that he ever did anything to address the poor man's longing and suffering; the rich man never points to any act of kindness on his part that might have **mitigated** his guilt.

These men could not have been more different. One was rich; the other was poor. One feasted while the other starved. One was clothed in purple; the other was covered in sores. The nameless "rich man" was unconcerned to keep the law of God because he had enough money to meet all of his needs; the other man had nothing except a name, Lazarus, which means "God helps." But they did have one thing in common—the one thing that all human beings have in common: they died (**v 22**). Their radically disparate lives came to an identical conclusion. They died and went to meet their eternal fate.

And in those eternal fates, we see that the inequality of their lives on earth is carried into the afterlife. But surprisingly for Jesus' audience, their fortunes are reversed. Their lives still could not be more different, but now Lazarus is living the good life while the rich man suffers. After his death, angels carry the beggar to **Abraham**'s side, a way of speaking of the welcome that the faithful will receive in heaven. We hear no more about Lazarus in this parable, except that he is viewed from below at Abraham's side (**v 23**). His life

> Lazarus' name seemed a sick joke in this life, but it is perfect for his eternity.

of torment is over. For him, eternity will be filled with comfort (**v 25**) and unimaginable pleasures. His name seemed like a sick joke in this life, but it is perfect in light of his eternity.

The rich man, however, goes to Hades (the realm of the dead), where he is in torment (**v 23**) and agony (**v 25**). His life of wealth and power has conditioned him to being in charge, and so in his pride he attempts to boss people around, even in Hades! When he appeals to Abraham as his spiritual father (**v 24** and **v 27**), his request meets the same fate as so many of Lazarus' pleas during the earthly life of the two men. He might call Abraham "father," and Abraham might formally speak to him as "son" (**v 25**), but the rich man never cared to act much like a son of Abraham by keeping the law during his life, and so now in death he finds himself quite alone. And in any event, there is a chasm fixed between heaven and hell that would prevent Lazarus from traveling between the two places, even if Abraham were inclined to send him (**v 26**).

In this way, Jesus presses home the great spiritual danger of loving money. Remember that Jesus is speaking to the Pharisees, who loved money (**v 14**). And he has just told them that "what people value highly is detestable in God's sight" (**v 15**). People like the rich man value wealth and comfort over all. We might be tempted to think that wealth is a sign of God's favor and approval. But it turns out that what we value is not what God values; he treasures the one who trusts in him and who obeys him. And so this parable invites us to examine our relationship with our money and possessions. Does our generosity toward those in need reflect a heart that loves God and his ways? Or are our hearts so fixed on our wealth that we are receiving all of our good things in this life (**v 25**—see 6:24 and 12:21)?

Listen!

Hearing that he will not receive any relief for his suffering, the formerly rich man gives up pleading his own lost cause and asks for a word of warning to be extended toward his five brothers so that they might avoid his fate (**16:27-28**). Abraham's response (**v 29**, in an echo of **v 16-17**) presses home the sufficiency and importance of God's word. The five brothers do not need a special visitor, for they have already received a supernatural revelation of God's will. Moses and the Prophets (again, a shorthand for the whole of the Old Testament Scriptures) speak to them about everything they need to know in order to avoid their brother's fate.

The rich man argues that something more extraordinary is required—if someone from the dead spoke to them, then they would repent (**v 30**) and presumably show the kind of love for the poor that the law requires. But Abraham corrects him—the problem is not that they do not know what to do. The problem is not that the brothers lack a compelling witness to the truth; they have Moses and the Prophets. The problem is that their hearts are hard (see **v 13-15**); even the appearance of someone from the dead would not have the power to change that fact (**v 31**).

Luke has recorded twin warnings about the dangers of wealth (6:24-25; 12:13-21) and also the necessity of responding to God's word with obedience (6:46; 8:15, 18, 21). Like the rich man's brothers, we have all of the revelation that we need in the Scriptures. We are not lacking instruction about how we ought to think about money and riches. The only question is whether we are listening.

Questions for reflection

1. How has this section helped you to have the same view of God's law that Jesus does?

2. If we do not have a clear view of the reality that real people go to a real hell, what difference does that make to us in the here and now?

3. What is one thing you need to think about, pray about, or get on with doing as a result of Jesus' teaching here?

6. KINGDOM COME, KINGDOM COMING

It will be easier to apply the lessons of the opening section of chapter 17 (v 1-19) if we first tackle the more complex teaching that follows it (v 20-35).

By now we have grown used to the Pharisees approaching Jesus with false or ulterior motives (e.g. 6:1-5), and so it comes as a bit of surprise in **17:20** that the Pharisees seem to be asking Jesus an honest question about when the kingdom would arrive. At that point in history, many of the promises that God had made to his people in the Old Testament seemed to be still unfulfilled. God had promised Abraham that he would bless the entire world through his descendants (see Genesis 12:2-3), but Israel was not in a place spiritually, politically, or culturally to be a blessing to anyone. God had promised **David** that the throne of his offspring would be established forever (2 Samuel 7:13), but Romans garrisons were stationed in Jerusalem with no potential king from David's line in sight. We are not at the same point in history, but perhaps we sometimes find ourselves asking the same question: when will God's promises be realized?

Jesus' preaching of the "good news of the kingdom" (referred to in Luke 4:43; 8:1; 16:16) was the news that God's promises were being realized in his arrival. Jesus' ministry of teaching, healing, and **exorcism** seemed to herald the arrival of an era of fulfillment; God was keeping his promises and everything would be different. But many Jews in that day expected that when the kingdom of God came, the enemies of God's people would be destroyed immediately and a new world would be ushered in (see Isaiah 65:17-25). Jesus' ministry met some of those expectations, but it certainly did not represent the cataclysmic upheaval that many anticipated (remember that even John the Baptist was confused by this dynamic, see Luke 7:18-28). Instead, the kingdom was small at the beginning, more like a mustard seed or a bit of yeast (13:18-21). It was present in the person of Christ, but it was also still something to be earnestly prayed for (11:2).

Jesus' response in Luke **17:20** indicates that the Pharisees were asking about potential signs of that kingdom's coming that would be observable in the physical world. But the kingdom cannot be located by careful observation, either of the earth or the stars, because it is "within you" (**v 21**). That Greek phrase (*entos humone estin*) can be translated as "within you" (as the NIV1984 does), giving the sense that the kingdom of God is found to be present internally in the individual who has embraced Jesus as the King sent by God. It can also be translated as "in your midst" (as the NIV2011 does—ESV renders it, "in the midst of you"), with the meaning that Jesus himself was the embodiment of the kingdom. The latter translation is most likely correct, for it seems highly unlikely that Jesus was encouraging the Pharisees to see themselves as possessing the kingdom. Geerhardus Vos comments on this verse:

> "Our Lord means to teach the enquirers that, instead of a future thing to be fixed by **apocalyptic** speculation, the coming of the kingdom is a present thing, present in the very midst of those who are curious about the day and hour of its sometime appearance."   (*The Teachings of Jesus Concerning the Kingdom of God and the Church*, page 53)

Don't Be Fooled

In **verse 22**, Jesus pivots from telling the Pharisees that the kingdom is a present reality to instructing his disciples about the reality of the future kingdom. They will "long to see one of the days of the Son of Man," a reference to Jesus' return to earth in splendor to judge God's enemies and vindicate his people. That longing will not be fulfilled in the short term ("you will not see it"), and therefore the disciples should not give credence to any reports that they might hear to the effect that Jesus is back (**v 23**).

Instead, the coming of "the Son of Man in his day" will be dramatic and visible to all, much like a flash of lightning (**v 24**). It will be an event impossible to miss, or to misunderstand; this seems to be the meaning of the curious expression in **verse 37**. When asked where these things would happen, Jesus replied, "Where there is a dead body, there

> The return of Jesus will be an event impossible to miss or to misunderstand.

the vultures will gather." That is to say, it is easy to locate a corpse when you see vultures swarming around it. In the same way, the events surrounding Jesus' return will not be difficult to see.

Because it will come suddenly and decisively (**v 34-35**), people will be caught unaware by the arrival of God's judgment. They will be going about their normal daily lives on the day that the Son of Man is revealed, and they will perish like the people in Noah's day (**v 26-27**) and in the days of Lot (**v 28-29**). "It will be just like this on the day the Son of Man is revealed" (**v 30**). There will be no opportunity to make preparations once that day has arrived (**v 31**); they must not fail to obey the Lord's instructions as Lot's wife did (**v 32**—see Genesis 19:26). Just as she should not have allowed the comforts of home to distract her from the urgency of the Lord's deliverance, so we must not be so enamored of the pleasures of our daily routine that we fail to follow Jesus with our whole hearts and lives. In light of that reality, Jesus repeats his call to discipleship in Luke **17:33**: "Whoever tries to keep their life will lose it, and whoever loses their life will preserve it" (see 9:24).

Life in the "Already/Not Yet"

That call to discipleship provides the framework into which the rest of the chapter fits. Jesus' followers must wrestle with what it looks like to live now in a way that makes sense of twin facts:

- The kingdom has already come in the person of Christ, bringing forgiveness and new spiritual life by virtue of his suffering (**17:25**) and resurrection.

- But there is a very real way that the kingdom of God has not yet come in its fullness. We still await Jesus' return.

Six principles for living in the "already/not yet" tension of the kingdom emerge from verses 1-19.

1. Jesus' followers must be watchful (**v 3**). In this fallen world, there will be temptations to sin (**v 1**). When Jesus comes back, sin will be eradicated and we will no longer have to endure daily temptations to sin, but for now, living in the times and places that we do, temptations abound. It is such a pervasive reality that we barely need to mention it; the advertising industry and the economic systems that are built on it all depend on tempting you to some degree of greed, envy, gluttony, and lust. Temptations to sin are everywhere, and so the Lord tells his disciples to be on guard.

2. In such a world, we also must be careful not to tempt others to sin. Jesus warns of a terrible fate for those who cause others to sin (**v 2**). As followers of Jesus, we must love others enough to examine our lives and our behaviors to make sure that we do not lead them into temptation. When someone speaks bitter, sarcastic, or lewd words, they tempt others to join them in their sin. When someone dresses provocatively or shows off their wealth in ostentatious ways, they risk being the cause of sinful responses in the hearts of their brothers and sisters.

3. Beyond the negative responsibility to not cause our brothers and sisters to sin, we also have a positive responsibility to rebuke them when they do sin (**v 3**). As followers of Jesus, our kingdom

commitment to righteousness means that we have an obligation to confront sin in the lives of other believers, particularly when our brother or sister sins against us. Obviously, that confrontation needs to be undertaken with a spirit of love and humility (see Galatians 6:1), but merely turning a blind eye to sin misses an opportunity to promote holiness in the individual and unity in the community of disciples.

4. Life in the "already/not yet" of the kingdom also requires Jesus' followers to forgive one another (Luke **17:3b-4**). Because this world is still fallen and not yet made new, your brothers and sisters in the church are still going to sin against you. Even if they sin against you and come back to repent seven times (an expression used in those days to communicate the sense of "no matter how many times"), you must forgive them.

   Forgiveness can be extremely difficult and painful. When someone has hurt you badly, giving up your "right" to be angry and vengeful can feel like yet another violation. But this dynamic is one of the ways that we live out the presence of the gospel of the kingdom in our lives. If the Son of Man suffered many things (**v 25**), paying the cost so that we could be forgiven for our sins, then we must be people who forgive those who sin against us. In the end, every sin will be paid for, either by Jesus on the cross or by individuals when Jesus returns to give justice (**18:7**). And so we do not need to get justice for ourselves; someone who does not forgive does not understand the gospel.

5. Jesus' followers should be characterized by humility. We should not allow any growth or progress in godliness, whether it is resisting temptation or rebuking and forgiving, to become a source of pride or self-satisfaction. In a brief comparison with the relationship between a master and his servants (**17:7-10**), Jesus reminds his disciples that such things are simply what is expected from them. Just as a master is not obligated to serve or thank his servants, so disciples should not imagine that their obedience

somehow puts God in their debt or earns some extra measure of his approval. The fact is that God is incredibly kind and gracious to his servants, but that love and care is rooted in his character, not in their performance. When they fail to obey him, they find their master forgiving. When they do obey, they have only done what they should do as faithful servants. That humble attitude gives glory to God, where it belongs.

6. Finally, kingdom citizens should be characterized by gratitude. In the account of the lepers' healing (**v 11-19**), we have a picture of the way the gospel works in our lives. Leprosy was a terrible disease, and those who were afflicted with it were required to stand at a distance (**v 12**) lest they infect healthy people. The surprise of the story lies both in the fact that only one person returned to show gratitude for the healing that he received (**v 15**), and especially that the one person who did return was a **Samaritan** (**v 16**). There is clearly more going on than mere physical healing, for all ten lepers received that gift. But this man alone had faith, and so he was the one who was made well spiritually (the Greek word used in **verse 19** is literally "saved").

If the message of the gospel of the kingdom is that Jesus' followers have been cleansed from a far more terrible pollution (sin) than leprosy, then it is only appropriate for them to be grateful people. Christians should live lives of genuine gratitude to God for what we have received; if you find it lacking in your life, take time each day to contemplate the incredible cost that Jesus paid so that your sins could be forgiven.

What You Need

The apostles' request for increased faith (**v 5**) follows directly on Jesus' insistence that they live lives of watchful righteousness (**v 1-4**), and rightly so, for the demands of the kingdom (and the leadership that the apostles will have to exercise in the community of believers) will require great faith in God and the good news of his kingdom. Jesus has already employed the image of a mustard seed (13:18-19) to explain the nature of the kingdom, and here it again serves as an example of something quite small that contains greater potential than we might imagine, for, "If you have faith as small as a mustard seed, you can say to this mulberry tree, 'Be uprooted and planted in the sea,' and it will obey you" (**17:6**).

We are not meant to put Jesus' words to the test by trying to relocate shrubbery using nothing but our faith. Those seeking to "prove" their faith through such dramatic signs have more in common with magicians and street charlatans than with the apostles' ministry of preaching, teaching, and healing:

> "The point is clear. Christians, even apostles, are distinguished not by the quantity of faith, but by the employment of faith; not by the greatness or smallness of faith, but by acting on faith, even faith the size of a mustard seed."
>
> (Edwards, *The Gospel According to Luke*, page 479)

While we certainly ought to long for greater faith because the Lord is honored by our trust, we should not imagine that we should delay obedience and service until faith is increased.

Faith is key to living in the "already/not yet" of the kingdom. Faith looks back to the incarnation and crucifixion and resurrection of Jesus, and sees the way that every one of God's promises have already become a "Yes" for us in him (2 Corinthians 1:20). Faith also looks forward to the return of the Son of Man as the day when all of the promises of God will be fulfilled completely. Faith grabs hold both of what God has done and what he has said he will do, and lives accordingly.

> Faith grabs hold both of what God has done and what he has said he will do, and lives accordingly.

Questions for reflection

1. What happens to our faith and expectations of life if we live as though:

   - the kingdom is already here, right now, in all its fullness?

   - the kingdom will never arrive in all its fullness?

2. Which of the six principles for now-but-not-yet living most encouraged you?

3. Which of those six principles most challenged you?

PART TWO

Chapter 18 contains six separate units, each introduced by Luke with some sort of statement of context or purpose. Every section both stands on its own as a rich teaching and also echoes the themes and ideas we have already seen in chapter 17.

A Powerless Widow

We have seen that discerning the main point of Jesus' parables can sometimes require a lot of careful work, but **18:1** is an interpreter's dream come true. Though the details of the so-called Parable of the **Importunate** Widow can be challenging, we are not left to guess what effect Jesus wished to have on his disciples: they should always pray and not give up.

The story is sketched out for us in vague terms; we are introduced to an unnamed judge and an unnamed widow who live in an un-named town (**v 2-3**). The widow has an adversary against whom she needs "justice," but we are not told the nature of her trouble. The judge has little incentive to assist the widow in this matter, for he "nei-ther feared God nor cared what people thought," and so "for some time he refused" (**v 4**). At last he is persuaded to get justice for her not for reasons of altruism or nobility, but because he has been worn down and frightened by her persistence (**v 5**).

If we are surprised by the judge's cynicism and selfishness, we must be shocked when Jesus ("the Lord") instructs his followers to listen to the judge (**v 6**). What possible lesson could we be meant to learn from this man? Jesus here argues from the lesser to the greater; if this lazy and indifferent judge can be prevailed upon by persistent **petition**, how much more will God "bring about justice for his chosen ones, who cry out to him day and night?" (**v 7**). The point is that God is much better than the unjust judge, and so if the judge secures justice for the widow, we can be certain that the heavenly Father will make sure that those who cry out to him get justice, and quickly (**v 8**). Snod-grass points out that:

> "The parable presupposes that people praying are in a much more advantageous relation to a righteous God who loves and hears his elect than the widow is to the unrighteous and uncaring judge." (*Stories With Intent*, page 457)

Luke's placement of this parable allows it to serve as a bridge between the teachings of chapter 17 and all that follows it in chapter 18. In context, it is not about persistence in prayer generally (though that is a good thing and perhaps a secondary implication of the text), for Jesus concludes the lesson with a question about his return: will the Son of Man find faith when he comes (**18:8**)? Luke's comment in **verse 1** is specifically referring to prayer regarding the return of Jesus. Readers have been warned about the danger of going about daily life unaware of Christ's imminent return (17:26-35). Instead, disciples should long to see that day (**v 22**), and so persist in steadfast prayer for Jesus' return and all the justice he will bring for his people.

A Proud Pharisee and a Humble Traitor

Just like the previous parable, the parable about the two men in the temple hinges on prayer. We are introduced to two characters who occupied the opposite ends of the social spectrum: a Pharisee and a tax collector (**18:10**). The Pharisees were widely respected for their piety and devotion to the **Torah**, and this particular man's religious rigor (as described in **verse 12**, and we have no reason to doubt his truthfulness) exceeded that which God required of his people in the Law of Moses. Tax collectors in Judea, on the other hand, were widely despised as traitors, thieves, and oppressors of their own people.

When these two men ascend the temple mount in order to pray, the basis on which they approach God is as starkly divergent as their social status. The Pharisee thanks God that he is better than other people, especially the tax collector (**v 11**), and points to his résumé of righteous deeds performed (**v 12**). The tax collector, however, approaches prayer with a posture of humility: he "stood at a distance," refused even to look into heaven, and beat his breast while crying out to God to be merciful to a sinner like him (**v 13**). As many commentators have pointed out, the man's plea for mercy should be understood as linked to the temple and its system of sacrifices for forgiveness. He is asking for God's mercy not on the basis of his own goodness (for he has very little), but on God's commitment to be merciful to sinners through the sacrifices taking place in the temple. This will be particularly significant in light of our consideration of **verses 31-34**.

This parable is meant to answer the implicit question: who is really righteous in God's sight? Who is truly part of his kingdom? The parable is told to "some who were confident of their own righteousness and looked down on everyone else" (**v 9**; see 7:39). While we may not feel that this describes our attitude toward God, the assumption of most religious people today is that, on some level, God's ultimate approval of us is based on our personal obedience and good deeds. If you tell this story to a Muslim or Buddhist friend (without the context of **18:9** and **14**), in my experience it is very likely they will assume that the Pharisee is the hero of the story, the one who goes home **justified** before God. After all, he is doing all the right things!

> Whenever we feel God does not love us because we have failed, we have adopted the Pharisee's approach.

This is why so many religious people are intolerably proud and judgmental; their scheme of justification-by-good-works means that what really counts in this world is how hard you work and how well you perform. Even Christians are not immune to the Pharisee's mindset. Whenever we create our own **extra-biblical** rules and judge other Christians who do not follow them, we are acting like a Pharisee. Whenever we feel that God does not love us because we have sinned or failed, we have adopted the Pharisee's approach.

Whenever we are proud of our own goodness, we are acting just like the Pharisee.

The tendency to **works-righteousness** is deeply ingrained in each of us. As a result, it is hard to overstate how shocking and revolutionary Jesus' conclusion is: the justified one is the sinner who approaches God on the basis of his mercy, rather than the "good" man who approaches God on the basis of his own merit. Jesus is destroying the fundamental principle of pretty much every religion! The pride and self-exaltation that would dare to hold up our own goodness as reason for God's love will lead to a terrible humbling, but "those who humble themselves will be exalted" (**v 14**; see Proverbs 3:34 and James 4:6, 10).

People Bringing Babies to Jesus

The next episode carries on the theme of humility and lowliness from the previous parable. Modern Western societies tend to idealize childhood as a time of innocence and trustworthiness, but this sensibility was unknown in Jesus' day. Speaking of these verses, Edwards writes that…

> "One will search ancient literature in vain for sympathy towards the young comparable to that shown them by Jesus."
> (*The Gospel According to Luke*, page 507)

Children were right next to tax collectors in terms of people with whom an important rabbi would never think to concern himself. But the **tense** of the verb in Luke **18:15** indicates that it was a recurring event for people to bring their babies to Jesus. The people's intention was that Jesus should place his hands on the babies, presumably to bless them and communicate a sense of personal care.

The disciples rebuked the people, perhaps out of a well-intentioned desire to protect Jesus' time and prestige. But Jesus seized the opportunity as an object lesson. The little children should not be hindered from coming to him, "for the kingdom of God belongs to such as these" (**v 16**). Not only are children legitimate candidates to come to Jesus and thus possess the kingdom, but in fact no one can enter the kingdom unless they do so "like a little child" (**v 17**).

The danger here is that we interpret Jesus' words too romantically. He is not saying that children are so innocent and lovely that they are worthy of the kingdom of God (or, as some have understood this passage, that they should be baptized); quite the opposite. The quality that children possess in abundance is their unworthiness; like the tax collector in **verses 9-14**, they had no résumé of spiritual accomplishments to tempt them to the works-righteousness that marked the Pharisee. One of the surprises of the kingdom of God is that it is those kinds of people, and only those kinds of people, who enter into it.

The Rich and Righteous Ruler

If the children remind us of the tax collector's unworthiness, the ruler of **verses 18-25** reminds us of the Pharisee in the temple. He had a lot going for him, spiritually speaking. He was wealthy (**v 23**), which both would have enabled him to give alms generously (see **v 12**) and also would have been interpreted as a sign of God's favor (hence the disciples' astonishment in **verse 26**). He was also a keeper of the law from his youth (**v 20-21**), a claim that Jesus does not bother to dispute. But despite those reasons to feel good about his spiritual state, he still comes to Jesus with some question about what else he must do to inherit eternal life (**v 18**). Notice that a works-righteousness approach always leads to anxiety, for we will never know whether we have done enough to please God in an ultimate way! In fact, both Roman Catholics and Muslims agree in their view that it is the highest presumption to imagine that we can know for certain that we have eternal life. If it is true that our good works are part of what merits God's favor, then they are absolutely correct. But, thanks be to God, that is the exact opposite of the good news of the kingdom.

Though Jesus does not directly challenge the man's claim to have kept the law since he was a boy, he does two things to undermine the man's efforts to earn eternal life by his own righteousness. First, in verse 19 he has pointed out that no one is good except God alone. Though Jesus deflects the man's flattery by questioning why he calls him good, his point is not to deny his own divinity or sinlessness. Instead, his goal is to focus the man on the goodness of God, a holiness and perfection that the ruler could never hope to attain by his own personal obedience or righteousness.

The second way that Jesus undermines the man's confidence in his own goodness is to call him to the radical self-sacrifice that the gospel of the kingdom demands (**v 22**—see 9:23-25 and 14:27). In this man's case, Jesus required him to sell all of his possessions, give to the poor, and then follow him. We should understand this not as a universal instruction to all followers of Christ (note that in the next chapter, Zacchaeus will sell only half of his possessions in response to Jesus' call, 19:8). Instead, Jesus the master surgeon is making a laser-focused application of 14:33 to this particular man, who loved money very much. Others are required to renounce other things—prestige, comfort, or family—but all must want the kingdom to the point that they would lose everything else in order to have it (see Matthew 13:44-46). That is why it is hard for the rich to enter the kingdom; the more possessions we have, the greater their gravitational pull on our hearts. For the wealthy, the narrow door of Luke 13:24 has now been reduced to the width of the eye of a needle (**18:25**).

> The more possessions we have, the greater their gravitational pull on our hearts.

How Can We Be Saved?

This entire section of Luke's Gospel is focused on disabusing us of the notion that we can be good enough to earn eternal life with God. But the disciples' question in **verse 26** is a good one—if being one of the "holy" people does not make one a citizen of the kingdom, who exactly can be saved? How do an unrighteous tax collector, an unimpressive child, and a helpless widow wind up as justified recipients of God's mercy?

The answer is that it is impossible, unless God does it (**v 27**). The answer to the puzzle of this chapter is there in **verses 31-33**. Jesus will fulfill "everything that is written by the prophets about the Son of Man" (**v 31**), particularly with respect to his suffering, death, and resurrection (**v 32-33**). That is how people with no righteousness of their own can be saved: not through their good works, but by virtue of Jesus' death in their place. On the cross, he took the guilt and shame and weakness of his people, so that when they cry out to God for mercy like the tax collector, they receive forgiveness and righteousness as a free gift (see 2 Corinthians 5:21).

The disciples did not understand what Jesus was talking about (Luke **18:34**), but they did have the self-renouncing faith that the ruler lacked (**v 28**). He was promised treasure in heaven (**v 22**), but would not part the treasures of the earth in order to gain it. But the disciples and all who share their faith in the promises of God are promised that they will gain far more (presumably, spiritual) blessings in this life, as well as the eternal life that the rich ruler so wanted desperately (though not as much as he wanted his money). Life is to be found in coming to Jesus with empty hands, not in walking away from him and grasping onto the things of this world.

The promise that Jesus makes in **verses 29-30** is a surprising conclusion to this conversation. We might expect that the Lord would offer his followers a choice between a good life now (the life that the ruler wanted so badly that he would not part with his wealth) and a good life in eternity. And in fact, following Jesus will mean sacrifice and difficulty in this life (**v 28-29**; see 6:22; 9:23-24). But Jesus says that not only will the one who makes sacrifices for the kingdom of God receive a reward in eternity, but that he or she will also "receive many times as much *in this age*" (**18:30**; italics mine). The Christian life is often difficult, but the gifts that we experience in the present (freedom from slavery to sin, membership in the family of God, fellowship with the people of God) far outweigh the benefits enjoyed by those who cling to their possessions and rebellion against God. Leaving all we have to follow the One who gives us everything offers more blessing, not only in the next life but also in this one.

Questions for reflection

1. How are your prayers shaped by the future coming of the kingdom?

2. In what ways is it easy for Christians to become like the Pharisee in the parable? When did you last simply say to God, "Have mercy on me, a sinner"?

3. How do verses 29-30 encourage you to be whole-hearted and sacrificial in your discipleship?

LUKE CHAPTER 18 VERSE 35 TO 19 VERSE 44

7. WHAT DO YOU WANT ME TO DO?

We have already been introduced to the road that connected Jerusalem to Jericho in Luke's Gospel—in the fictional story of the Good Samaritan (10:30-35)—but now Jesus is traveling that pathway in real life. The next section of the Gospel relates two separate interactions between Jesus and individuals who were in great need. We might understand if Jesus were preoccupied with the reality of his upcoming crucifixion, for the cross looms large over all of the events of the next chapters. But the Lord was journeying to Jerusalem for the express purpose of dying for his people, and he was not uncompassionate toward those who required his help.

A Blind Beggar

In **18:35**, Luke tells us that a blind man sat by the road begging. In those days there was no social security or unemployment insurance, and a blind person would probably be unable to find good work. In the absence of a family that could support him, someone with physical disabilities would most likely be reduced to begging in order to survive. This location would have been a strategic place to beg; pilgrims on their way to Jerusalem would have used this road, and so beggars would line the road hoping to receive some alms from the religious travelers.

On the day in question this blind man (who, Mark 10:46 reveals, was named Bartimaeus) hears the noise of a crowd (Luke **18:36**) and asks about what is happening. When is he told that Jesus of Nazareth is passing by (**v 37**), he creates quite a scene, calling out, "Jesus, Son of David, have mercy on me!" (**v 38**). This is the first time in Luke's Gospel that we hear someone use the term "Son of David" to refer to Jesus, but for reasons that we have already seen, it is a title that is loaded with meaning (see commentary on 9:20 in *Luke 1–12 For You*, pages 125-126). David was the great king of Israel in the Old Testament, and to call Jesus the "Son of David" was to express faith in him as the Messiah, God's long-promised King. And this blind man will not be put off confessing who Jesus is and asking him for his mercy by others' harsh words (**18:39**).

When he is finally brought to Jesus (**v 40**), the Son of David's question seems a bit obtuse: "What do you want me to do for you?" (**v 41**). It seems fairly obvious from both the context clue and also the man's repeated shouting that he wants Jesus to have mercy on him, particularly in the form of healing his blindness. But perhaps it is best to understand Jesus' question as his way of drawing the man out, giving him an opportunity to verbalize his trust in Jesus and make his request known to him.

If you stop to think about it, Jesus' question is a particularly searching one. The beggar's words are a simple expression of both his need and also his confidence that Jesus is the only one who can help him. Jesus healed him in response to his faith (**v 42**) and Bartimaeus "followed Jesus, praising God" along with "all the people" (**v 43**).

Small Man, Big Sinner

As Jesus passes through Jericho (**19:1**), Luke shows us yet another memorable encounter with a person in need. The need in Zacchaeus' life was perhaps less obvious than that of Bartimaeus, but it was even more pressing. He was a "chief tax collector" (**v 2**), meaning that he had grown quite rich by cheating and oppressing his fellow countrymen (**v 8**). Because we tend only to remember the memorable detail of Zacchaeus' small stature and his need to climb a tree in order to see Jesus (**v 3-4**), we can easily lose sight of the fact that he was not a cute or cuddly little man. He was a wildly successful thief and a traitor to his people; this was the kind of "sinner" (**v 7**) that seemed to be obviously outside of God's program of salvation. This was a man in deep need of mercy and forgiveness for his sins.

And that is exactly what Jesus brought to town. We do not know how Jesus knew Zacchaeus' name (was he that notorious?), but when he saw the man in a tree, he told him that he "must" stay at his house that day (**v 5**). The significance of this request was not lost on anyone—this was Jesus accepting Zacchaeus as one of his followers; this was nothing less than "salvation" coming to this man's house (**v 9**). The response of the people to this news splits along the lines that we have come to expect. Zacchaeus (the sinner) welcomed Jesus gladly and voluntarily amended his ways (**v 6** and **v 8**—see 2:10 and 13:17), while the people grumbled and muttered about Jesus' willingness to eat with sinners (**19:7**; see 15:2).

In a way, the stories of these two men serve as a conclusion to everything that precedes them in chapter 18. Like the infants brought to Jesus (18:15-17), Bartimaeus and Zacchaeus have no prestige or honor to bring to Jesus. Like the persistent widow (18:1-8), both men have to persist through obstacles in order to get what they want. Like the tax collector in the temple (18:9-14), both men have absolutely no hope except to cry out to Jesus for mercy. And unlike the rich ruler (18:18-30), Zacchaeus joyfully gave away his money (**19:8**) and Bartimaeus began to follow Jesus (**18:43**).

> Truly receiving the love of Jesus has a truly profound impact on people's lives.

Truly receiving the love of Jesus has a truly profound impact on people's lives. Both Bartimaeus and Zacchaeus had a dramatic encounter with Jesus, and the experience changed them. Before his healing, the blind man probably desperately wanted to see so that he could live a "normal" life. But once Jesus healed him, he did not use his new gift to go back home and make himself comfortable. Instead, he went to see the world as one of Jesus' followers. Before Jesus befriended him, Zacchaeus' life was committed to the pursuit of ill-gotten wealth. But once Jesus came into his life, he was transformed into a man who could joyfully give away half of his goods to those in need and make restitution to those he had wronged.

It must be that way for us as well. There is no such thing as a person who has truly encountered the love of Jesus and yet walked away unchanged. How strange it would have been if the blind man had wanted Jesus to heal him, but did not want Jesus to be his teacher and master! How pointless would Jesus' friendship be if it left Zacchaeus just as selfish and deceitful and greedy as before! The great thing about Jesus' love is that it transforms people and sets them free to love him back; it was so two thousand years ago and it is so today.

The Kind of Person Whom Jesus Loves

In the end, what perhaps should strike us most in these two interactions is the incredible love of Jesus. These are wretched, miserable people. But Jesus' compassion overflows for the blind man. He loves Zacchaeus the scandalous sinner even though they have never met. Jesus doesn't just tolerate him, but he actually invites himself over to Zacchaeus' house for the foreseeable future. In that culture, to break bread with someone was an act of fellowship, a sign of acceptance and identification and trust. In short, it meant that you were on good terms. Jesus is extending himself in friendship and love and acceptance to the tax collector.

This is radical love. You would have had to work hard to find a man more loathed in all of Israel than Zacchaeus. It is amazingly good news that when God's Son came in human flesh, his love was not reserved for the people who deserved it, but instead he pursued relationships with hard-core, beyond-the-pale sinners. No one would have expected that when God came to earth he would lavish his kindness on the very worst people, but he did!

And that is the only reason that we have any hope. You will never appreciate what Jesus has done until you see that either you are Bartimaeus, Zacchaeus, the persistent widow, and the tax collector in the temple or you are the Pharisee, the rich ruler, and the crowds condemning Zacchaeus. The only real difference between those two groups of people is that the former can see their need for Jesus clearly and the latter are blinded by their own self-righteousness. Both kinds of people are trapped in misery, either by virtue of their helplessness or their self-righteousness. Both kinds of people need Jesus, but only one kind of person is screaming by the side of the road and climbing up into a tree to get him. If you think that you deserve Jesus' love, you will not receive it. But if what you want most is his mercy and salvation, you will receive it as a free gift.

The Seeking, Suffering Shepherd

Jesus gives a concluding interpretation to the events in Jericho in **19:10**. The reason why salvation has come to the house of the unworthy Zacchaeus (the "for" at the start of the verse is a statement of purpose) is because "the Son of Man has come to seek and save the lost". Jesus is clarifying the nature and object of his mission along lines that we have already seen in Luke's Gospel (see 5:31-32; 15:7). Despite what we would naturally expect, wretched people like Zacchaeus are not outside the scope of his salvation. In fact, Jesus came for the express purpose of bringing salvation to those who, like the chief tax collector, had wandered from the faith of their father Abraham (**19:9**).

Jesus came to save the lost, and that means that he would have to seek them out. People who are lost, by definition, do not know how to get where they need to go. Spiritually lost people cannot find their way to God, and so God had to come and seek them out. That is exactly what Jesus did; he left his Father's side and all of the riches of heaven to step into our world and find his wandering sheep (see 15:3-5). God did not sit back and wait to see if humanity could grope in the darkness and somehow find him, but he sent his Son to live among us and seek and save the lost.

We are again meant to be reminded of how, back in the book of Ezekiel, the Lord condemned the leaders of Israel (the "shepherds") for their failure to care for the spiritual needs of God's people (the "sheep")—and how he declared that he would one day do the job himself. His promise bears repeating:

> "I myself will search for my sheep and look after them. As a shepherd looks after his scattered flock when he is with them, so will I look after my sheep. I will rescue them from all the places where they were scattered on a day of clouds and darkness ... I will search for the lost and bring back the strays. I will bind up the injured and strengthen the weak, but the sleek and the strong I will destroy. I will shepherd the flock with justice."
>
> (Ezekiel 34:11-12, 16)

Jesus brought salvation to Zacchaeus' house (Luke **19:9**) as a fulfillment of that promise.

And lest we forget, Jesus has just told us what this mission will cost him. He did not just pop in to seek and save the lost in the way that you and I might execute errands on a Saturday afternoon. Seeking and saving the lost meant that he would be delivered over to the Gentiles, who would mock him and treat him shamefully, spit upon him and flog him (18:32). He would be nailed to a cross and left to die (v 33) for the sins of lost people like Zacchaeus and Bartimaeus. He called Zacchaeus down from his tree on the way to climbing a very different tree. No wonder Jesus left people full of glory, praise, and joy (**18:43** and **19:6**)!

And if we are going to follow Jesus with joy and praise, we will have to love what he loved and pursue the same mission that he pursued. That means that we need to love lost people and we need to work to seek and save the lost. Instead of remaining at a judgmental distance (**v 7**), followers of Christ should cultivate love and sympathy for those trapped in their sins, and they should work to bring them into contact with the good news of Jesus.

Questions for reflection

1. "Truly receiving the love of Jesus has a truly profound impact on people's lives." How have you experienced this in your own life, and seen it in the lives of those around you?

2. How does reflecting on passages like this help us retain, or recapture, a sense of Jesus' overwhelming love for us personally?

3. Are there people around you who have given their lives to amassing wealth? Do you assume they would not see their need of the gospel—or do you see them as potential Zacchaeuses? How will you seek to share the gospel with them?

PART TWO

The famous Parable of the Ten Minas comes in a very specific historical situation. Jesus was approaching Jerusalem and people thought
that the kingdom of God was going to appear suddenly (**v 11**). As we
have seen in previous chapters, the tension between the "already" of
the kingdom and the "not yet" of the kingdom was a cause of great
confusion in Jesus' day. He had declared that salvation had come to
Zacchaeus' house that day (**v 9**), and his ministry of healing the sick
and giving sight to the blind were rightly interpreted as signs that the
kingdom was in their midst. But the crowds generally failed to understand that the kingdom would not come in its fullness immediately,
but would grow slowly toward a final consummation when Jesus returns (13:18-21). It was in this air of heightened expectations that
Jesus took the opportunity to tell the people a parable about the kingdom. In reality, the parable contains two different stories, one about
a nobleman and his interaction with his subjects (**19:12, 14, 27**), and
also a more detailed story about that nobleman's interaction with his
servants, to whom he had given some money to invest.

A Rejected King

The parable begins with an allusion to an incident that would have been
familiar to Jesus' audience. About thirty years earlier, before Herod the
Great had died, he had split up his mini-empire among his sons, giving
Judea and Samaria to his son Archelaus. But Herod's bequeathals were
ultimately subject to Roman approval, so Archelaus went off to Rome
to have Caesar Augustus approve his appointment.

Before he left, however, there was a riot in the temple at Passover and Archelaus had over 3,000 Jews slaughtered. The Jews of
Jerusalem and the surrounding areas had not much cared for Herod
the Great and his murderous ways (including, of course, his killing
of the boys of Bethlehem, Matthew 2:16), and they were even less
thrilled about the idea of being ruled by his son. So they dispatched a

delegation of 50 men to Rome to appeal to Caesar for a different king. They lost their appeal; Archelaus became king… and his palace was in Jericho, the town that Jesus had just walked through.

The echoes in the parable are clear. A man goes off to be appointed king (Luke **19:12**) but is pursued by a delegation of people who oppose the idea of him ruling over them (**v 14**). After all is said and done, the man receives his appointment and calls for his opponents to be slaughtered in front of him (**v 27**). In the same way, Jesus is about to take an extended trip of sorts in order to receive a kingdom. He is going to Jerusalem, where his kingship will be opposed by the Jewish leaders (see 23:1-5). In the end, he will return after an extended absence to inaugurate his kingdom, and there will be punishment for those who have resisted his rule (see 13:1-9).

Obviously, Jesus is not implying that he is a murderous despot like Archelaus! Instead, we should understand the parable to teach that if even mild opposition to a mid-level ruler results in punishment, how much more will opposing the true King of the universe result in devastation. This part of the story is a warning: opposing him will have awful consequences. Jesus is going to go away, and when he returns, **19:27** will become a reality on earth.

While the King is Gone

Most of the parable is dedicated to the events that took place while the master was away. The attention here turns from the nobleman's opponents to his ten servants, each of whom is given a mina, roughly three months' wages, to put to work in his absence (**v 13**). It is clear from the tone of the charge that the reckoning in **verse 15** was to be anticipated, and the servants' responses indicate that they were in fact fully expecting to give an account for their stewardship once their master came back.

The first servant has earned an astonishing eleven-fold return on his investment (**v 16**); the second servant a still-impressive five further minas (**v 18**). The master is pleased with the servants' performance and rewards them lavishly. Because they have been faithful with the mina they were given, they will be given entire cities to "take charge" of (**v 17, 19**). We can well imagine that a newly appointed king with quite a few enemies would need trustworthy men governing his cities, and these servants have proven themselves to be loyal. The reward they receive is extravagant in comparison to the faithfulness, but the principle that fidelity in small things translates to fidelity in much larger matters seems to be in the forefront of the nobleman's mind (**v 17**, see 16:10).

The other servant that is mentioned did not fare so well. In fact, he didn't even make an effort, but protected his mina in a piece of cloth (**19:20**). While that was an effective strategy for protecting what he had been given, he had been charged with putting the money to work (**v 13**). When he was called to give an account, this servant decided to defend himself by insulting his master: "I was afraid of you, because you are a hard man. You take out what you did not put in and reap what you did not sow" (**v 21**).

Nothing in the parable indicates that the master deserved this characterization (in fact he appears to be quite generous to his servants in **verse 17** and **verse 19**), or even that the servant genuinely believed it, but the master does not bother to defend himself. Instead he turns the man's words back on him, wondering why the servant would not seek to placate such a ruthless employer by giving him the return on investment that he expected (**v 22-23**). The money (and probably the city that goes with it) is taken from that servant and given to the one who already has ten (**v 24**). When the bystanders object (**v 25**), the nobleman tells them that this is the way that it works: those who prove faithful get even more; those who are faithless have even the little that they have taken away (**v 26**).

The parable seems to make two points. First, those who oppose Jesus' kingship will be met with judgment. Second, those who follow Jesus must be faithful in their service until he returns, for we will ultimately give an account for the way we have used what our master has given us (2 Corinthians 5:10; Revelation 22:12).

The details of the story probably do not allow us to **allegorize** each of the servants. On one hand, it seems as if the third servant might represent Christians who are not faithful with the opportunities God has given them. After all, he is a servant in the household of the master (not someone on the outside). But the way that the master condemns him as a wicked man seems incompatible with the believer's status in Christ. It is best to simply learn the lessons that the parable is meant to teach without attempting to apply every detail to our current situation.

The lesson of the parable seems to be: if you are a follower of Christ, every aspect of your life is a gift given to you for the purpose of investment. The place where you live, the job where you work, your weekends, the abilities and education that you have received, your money, your health, your family, your interactions with people who do not believe in Jesus, your suffering—all of it is given to you as a stewardship. You are not free to use those things for your own purposes or to neglect them all together. Too many Christians adopt the third servant's approach to the things that the Lord has given to them, lazily or foolishly failing to put them to use

> We will ultimately give an account for the way we have used what our master has given us.

toward the interests of their master. Instead, we must invest all that we have in the priorities and plans of Jesus (if you need a hint at what those are, look at Luke **19:10**). We all must live like servants who will give an account when the king returns.

Christians are those who have been brought into God's household completely by his grace, and made servants of light when we were enslaved in darkness. And now, through nothing of our own doing, God has promised to richly reward us for our service to him. Jesus repeatedly uses versions of this idea that those who have much will receive more, and those who have little will have it taken away from them (**v 26**; 8:18; Mark 4:25; and, in a parable very similar to that of the Ten Minas, Matthew 25:29). We might daydream of God's blessings in terms of riches and ease, but in those contexts we see that the reward is actually the opportunity to enjoy more fruitful service to and understanding of the Lord. As always, the greatest blessing the Lord gives to his people is more of himself!

The Welcome of the King

Luke's account of Jesus' "triumphal entry" into Jerusalem follows on the theme of kingship that was introduced in the parable that precedes it (Luke **19:28**). Just as the parable introduces us to a would-be king, Jesus approaches the city as "the king who comes in the name of the Lord" (**v 38**). His miraculous foreknowledge of the circumstances under which the disciples would find a colt for him to ride (**v 29-34**) demonstrates a...

> "sovereignty over all that 'must' transpire in Jerusalem ... Jesus' prescience increases in proportion to his proximity to the cross."
> (Edwards, *The Gospel According to Luke*, page 545)

Jesus' decision to ride in on a colt (a generic term for a male horse or donkey) is an intentional fulfillment of the prophecy of Zechariah 9:9-10, where the future king is portrayed as coming in humility, riding a colt and bringing peace:

> "Rejoice greatly, Daughter Zion!
> Shout, Daughter Jerusalem!
> See, your king comes to you,
> righteous and victorious,
> lowly and riding on a donkey,
> on a colt, the foal of a donkey.
> I will take away the chariots from Ephraim

and the warhorses from Jerusalem,
and the battle bow will be broken.
He will proclaim peace to the nations.
His rule will extend from sea to sea
and from the River to the ends of the earth."

The significance of Jesus' choice of mode of entry into the city was not lost on those who witnessed it. It is common to understand the choice of a donkey as a gesture of unusual humility, but the Old Testament rulers of Israel were known to ride such animals (see 1 Kings 1:38-40 and 2 Samuel 16:1-2). If the donkey has any symbolic significance, it is more likely as a gesture of a king coming in peace (as opposed to entering the city on a warhorse; see Revelation 19:11-16). The crowds understood that Jesus was entering the city like a king (Luke **19:38**) and the Pharisees did not approve (**v 39**).

The disciples threw their cloaks on the animal and "put Jesus on it" like a king on his throne (**v 35**). The people threw their cloaks on the ground in front of him (**v 36**), a first-century version of rolling out a red carpet. As the procession neared the Mount of Olives, the crowds began to live out the command of Zechariah 9:9 by joyfully praising God (Luke **19:37**) and hailing Jesus as "the king who comes in the name of the Lord" (**v 38**). Just as the heavenly host cried out praise to God when Jesus came as a baby (2:14), now the people declare, "Peace in heaven and glory in the highest!" as Jesus comes as the king (**19:38**).

The Real-Life Rejection of the King

Just as the king in the parable of the Ten Minas was opposed, so here the Pharisees call on Jesus to rebuke his enthusiastic disciples (**v 39**). Perhaps they have theological objections to Jesus being identified as the Messiah, or it could be that they fear that Rome will crack down on such a display of fervor. In any event, Jesus responds by saying that if the people are silenced, the stones will themselves cry out (**v 40**).

This should be understood ironically; Jesus is saying that even inanimate creation can sense what is happening here.

The joy of the entry narrative passes quickly, as is appropriate, given that Jesus is heading to the cross. In **verse 41** Jesus finally sees Jerusalem, marking the end of a journey that began back in 9:51, and he begins to weep for the city like one of the prophets of old (e.g. Jeremiah 9:1). Even though he has been warmly received, Jesus knows that most of the city's inhabitants will reject him. They will not recognize "the time of God's coming" to them (Luke **19:44**).

Jesus came to the city as a king on the way to a cross, bringing both salvation for those who would recognize his kingship and judgment for those who would oppose him. But Jerusalem did not know the things that make for peace (**v 42**), and so Jesus predicts the total destruction of the city in graphic terms (**v 43-44**) that call to mind the conclusion of the parable of the Ten Minas (particularly **verse 27**). These words did come to pass in AD 70, when the Roman army laid siege to Jerusalem and destroyed it along with the temple. Rejecting the king had (and has) a terrible consequence.

> Jesus came as a king on the way to a cross.

But in case we get a picture in our minds of Jesus as a vengeful tyrant, it is helpful to remember that he spoke these words because they were true, not because he was a sadist. Jesus wept over the terrible fate of the city. To be sure, his was not the sorrow of impotence; he was not saying, *Oh, how I wish there were something I could do about this!* In **verse 42** it is clear that the people couldn't see because the truth was being hidden from them; judgment had already been set. But Jesus' posture toward the rebellious city was one of compassion, for he does not perversely delight in the destruction of the wicked (see Ezekiel 33:11).

For those of us who follow Jesus, we should rejoice that God has sent us the King, and his Spirit has opened our eyes to see how we can have peace with him. But for us who follow Jesus, if we love the things that he loves, if we care about the things that he cares about, then we will have a similar response to his to people who persist in rejecting him. When God's judgment fell on Jerusalem in the form of the Roman army in AD 70, it was terrible (Luke **19:43-44**). When Jesus comes back and judges the whole earth, it will be far worse. If Jesus wept with compassion for the city, how much more should we weep over (and then go to) the nations who do not yet know Christ!

Questions for reflection

1. "If you are a follower of Christ, every aspect of your life is a gift given to you for the purpose of investment." Is that your perspective on your time, your talents, and your relationships?

2. For what kind of Christian is Jesus' parable a warning? For what sort of Christian is it a wonderful encouragement?

3. Are you more likely to make the mistake of celebrating judgment of sinners, or forgetting that there is a judgment at all? How would copying Jesus' compassion change your priorities this week?

8. SHOWDOWN AT THE TEMPLE

The whole direction of Luke's Gospel has been moving toward the cross (see 9:51), and now Jesus has entered the city that kills the prophets (13:33-34). The next two chapters take place during the Passover season in the temple complex, where Jesus will teach daily until he is arrested. As the temple is the center of the Jewish religious life of which Jesus was so critical, it is fitting that the final climactic showdowns of his earthly ministry should take place here at the temple.

Cleansing the Temple

Luke's account of the cleansing of the temple is much shorter than those of the other Gospel writers, as his version leaves out the overturning of the money changers' tables (Matthew 21:12). Jesus entered into the temple courts (Luke **19:45**), particularly the outer court where Gentiles were permitted to mix with the Jewish worshippers. The **Sadducees** oversaw this region of the temple, and the changing of money and the selling of animals for sacrifices was a huge stream of revenue for the temple.

But Jesus was outraged by the naked profiteering of "those who were selling" (**v 45**), and as he drove them out, he compared their work to that of robbers (**v 46**). The first part of the quote in this verse comes from Isaiah 56:7, and in context there the Lord is seeing a day when all peoples, both Jews and Gentiles, will be able to bring acceptable worship to him. But at the Jerusalem temple, the place where sacrifices were brought and worship was offered, the system of buying and selling had turned God's house into a den of robbers (quoting now from Jeremiah 7:11).

This was a gesture pregnant with meaning; Jesus essentially stormed in and staged a coup in the temple. He kicked out the old system and then proceeded to hold court for the next five days, teaching a rapt audience that "hung on his words" (Luke **19:47-48**). The religious leaders, including "the chief priests, the teachers of the law, and the leaders among the people" all understood the significance of what was happening. The only thing keeping them from killing Jesus was the adoration of the crowds.

A Question of Authority

On a subsequent day as Jesus was preaching the good news, the elders and chief priests confronted him about the authority by which he was doing "these things" (**20:1-2**). This was the one place where they probably felt that they could press an advantage over Jesus. He was wildly popular (**19:48**), but he did not have a title or position. Jesus was outside of the religious and political establishment, and so in the eyes of the leaders he had no credentials or pedigree to justify his cleansing of the temple and his ministry of teaching and healing.

Jesus did not answer them directly, but instead he turned the matter around and asked them a question about the authority that lay behind John's baptism: "Was it from heaven, or of human origin?" (**20:3-4**). This was a strategically brilliant question for two reasons. First, it effectively trapped the leaders into answering their own question, for John had testified clearly that Jesus was the Messiah, the anointed King sent by God to save his people (3:15-22; see John 1:19-35). If the leaders acknowledged that John's authority was from heaven (that is, from God), then Jesus could simply tell them to listen to what John said about him. He had the authority to cleanse the temple because he was the Messiah. But if they said that John's authority was not of divine origin, then it would be obvious that they were not in a position where they would be willing to acknowledge Jesus's authority. In forcing the leaders to take a position on John, Jesus was forcing them to take a position on his ministry; he was essentially making them answer the question they asked him.

The second aspect of its brilliance was that it put the leaders on the horns of a political dilemma, a fact that they acknowledged in Luke **20:5-6**. They obviously could not admit that John's ministry was from God, for that would open them to rebuke since they had not believed him (**v 5**) nor honored him as a prophet. But they were also afraid of the people. The people were persuaded that John was a prophet and apparently the people had rocks that they were willing to throw (**v 6**). So the religious leaders didn't dare say anything negative about him.

It is indicative of the spiritual condition of these leaders that the truth was far less important to them than the political ramifications of the truth. As a result, they chose to take the least damaging route and simply told Jesus that they did not know how to answer to his question (**v 7**). They came to undermine Jesus' authority, but they were the ones who had been exposed as woefully inadequate to exercise leadership over God's people. If they would not answer Jesus' question with integrity, they would not receive an answer from Jesus (**v 8**).

The Parable of the Vineyard

The tension in this moment must have been so thick that you could cut it with a knife. The people were hanging on Jesus' every word (**19:48**) but the religious establishment literally wanted to kill him. Now just when they thought they had Jesus cornered with a question about his authority, they found themselves publicly humiliated by his response. Most people in this situation would want to change the subject or say something conciliatory in order to defuse the tension. Jesus, however, was not most people. Instead of trying to pacify the angry leaders, he turned to the crowd (**20:9**) and told a parable that was clearly meant to skewer the scribes and chief priests (**v 19**).

The parable recounts the relationship between a man who planted a vineyard and the tenant-farmers to whom he rented it (**v 9**). This was a fairly common business relationship in those days , wherein the farmers would work the land and pay their rent with a share of the fruit. When the owner, who had gone away "for a long time" (**v 9**), sent a servant to collect the rent that he was owed, "the tenants beat him and sent him away empty-handed" (**v 10**). We are not told what motivated their actions, but it seems they understood the landlord's absence as an opportunity for them to assert themselves and their interests over and against him and his.

The owner responded with amazing patience, sending a second and then a third servant, each of whom received the same scandalous treatment (**v 11-12**). At that point, he decided to send his beloved son in the hope that they might show him more respect than they had shown to the servants (**v 13**). The tenants, however, saw their chance to kill the son and take ownership of the vineyard for themselves (**v 14-15**). It seems that they misinterpreted the son's appearance as a sign that the owner had died, and so if they were able to eliminate the man who stood to inherit the property, they might be able to assert something like our concept of "squatter's rights."

This was, however, a drastic miscalculation. They assumed that the owner was either dead or feeble, or lacked the will to oppose them, but they could not have been more wrong. Jesus ends the parable in **verse 16** by saying that the tenants will be destroyed and the fields they have tried to steal will be given over to other tenants.

The parable opens up neatly along allegorical lines, and the immediate responses of the audience (**v 16** and **v 19**) show that the meaning of the parable was transparent to them. The vineyard is an image used in the Old Testament to represent the nation of Israel (e.g. Isaiah 5:1-7; Psalm 80:8-18). This would mean that the tenants of the parable are the leaders of Israel: namely, the chief priests, the scribes, the Pharisees, and the Sadducees. It was their job to tend the vineyard of God's people, to work to help it produce spiritual fruit for the Lord. The servants that are sent to collect the proceeds are the prophets, who called on the people of Israel to produce the obedience and justice and worship that they owed to the Lord. The people of Israel systematically mistreated God's prophets (see Luke 11:47-51 and 13:34), and now in just a few short days this generation would make matters worse by killing God's Son.

The primary point of that parable was not merely to reflect on the history of Israel, but rather, to explain that the leaders of Israel were going to be removed from office by the Lord. They would be replaced by followers of Jesus. The scribes and elders did not miss the meaning of Jesus' parable, and they were outraged by it (**20:19**). But Jesus looked right at them and in **verse 17** responded to their objection with a quotation from Psalm 118.

This seems likes seem like an abrupt change of subject. After all, they have been talking about vineyards and messengers and sons, and now suddenly the topic has shifted to builders and stones. But most likely there is a play on words at work here. The words for "son" and "stone" in He-

> Jesus is the cornerstone on which people are built or broken.

brew and Aramaic (which is most likely the language Jesus was speaking) are similar (*ben* and *eben*, respectively). And so it is likely that Jesus is creating a play on words and mixing his metaphors. He tells a story about a rejected son (*ben*) and then quotes a psalm about a rejected stone (*eben*). Jesus is both the Son of God and the cornerstone on which the people of God are built (Luke **20:17**), and on which the enemies of God are broken (**v 18**).

When the parable and the quotation from Psalm 118 are put together, we see that the leaders of Israel are like both the tenants who rejected the owner's son and also the builders who rejected the most important stone. In rejecting Jesus and his ministry, the leaders of Israel were missing out on the thing that they needed most. They were like builders who were tasked with creating a building but who had foolishly rejected the one stone that was crucial to holding the whole structure together.

On the most basic level, this parable and the quotation from Psalm 118 that comes with it are not aimed at followers of Christ; they are aimed at the leaders of Israel in Jesus' day that rejected him. But there are principles at work in the teaching that we can import into our circumstance. If you think about it, the tenants' most basic crime was that they were acting as if they should be the owners (and not the caretakers) of the vineyard. Instead of using the land for the benefit of the owner, they wanted to use it for their own selfish purposes.

That dynamic is a powerful picture of what sin looks like in your life. God has given you all kinds of resources: family, friends, intelligence, personality qualities, experiences, spiritual gifts, health, etc. If you occupy a position of leadership in the church, you have been given a precious responsibility. And you were given all of those things in order to serve God, to bear fruit for him. But sin tempts us to live our lives as if we are the owners of all of these things, not the tenants. Sin is living as if we make the rules in God's vineyard, putting all the means of production to work serving ourselves. In the terms of this parable, sin is most basically acting as if you are the owner when you are really the tenant.

Questions for reflection

1. Why is it right that our treatment of Jesus is the basis on which God's judgment is meted out to us?

2. How does seeing sin in the context of the parable of the vineyard motivate you to fight your sin?

3. What alternative cornerstones do we seek to build our lives upon?

PART TWO

Undaunted by repeated failures to outsmart or outmaneuver Jesus, the religious leaders resolved to keep "a close watch on him," sending spies to try and catch Jesus saying something that would justify handing him over to the authorities (Luke **20:20**). Needless to say, their plan did not work out as they had hoped...

Taxes , Teachers, and a Gift in the Temple

After a bit of particularly dripping and disingenuous flattery (**v 21**), the spies' first attempt to trap Jesus revolved around the issue of taxes: should the Jewish people pay taxes to Caesar or not (**v 22**)? This most likely was a question about the imperial **poll tax** that had been instituted by Rome about twenty years earlier. The amount that the citizens of Jerusalem were required to pay for the tax was one denarius, basically a day's wage for a laborer. As you can well imagine, such a tax was still a sore subject.

The goal of the spies' question, then, was to force Jesus into taking a position that would entrap him. If, on one hand, Jesus said that people should not pay the tax, then the scribes and priests could report him to the Romans, who did not hesitate to eliminate anyone who might seem like a threat to the peace of the empire. But if, on the other hand, he said that they should pay the tax, then he might well be seen as a traitor by the people of Israel. There was a large group of people in Jerusalem who wanted to start a revolution against Rome, and at least some of them were looking to Jesus to start the ball rolling. The approval of the people was the only thing keeping the leaders from making a move on Jesus, so if Jesus said something wildly unpopular, then the religious leaders might gain the upper hand that they so desperately wanted.

Luke's comment in **verse 23** makes it clear that Jesus understood what they were trying to do to him, and his response manages to both answer their question and outfox them in the game they are playing. In one sense he affirms the authority of Caesar. He calls for the coin that is used to pay the tax, he observes the image of the emperor on it, and he tells people that it is appropriate to use such a coin to pay such a tax. This is right in line with what the Bible tells us about our relationship to the government authorities (Romans 13:1-2 and 1 Peter 2:13-17—and remember, Paul and Peter lived in societies that were ruled by some corrupt and ruthless men). Followers of Christ should be law-abiding citizens wherever they live (unless obeying the law of man would require someone to disobey God—see Acts 5:29), and that includes paying taxes.

But in another sense, though Jesus affirms the validity of Caesar's authority, there is also a dismissiveness in his response. He calls for the denarius and asks whose "image and inscription" are on it (Luke **20:24**). The coin in question would have had Tiberius Caesar's image on it and have borne the inscription, "Tiberius Caesar Augustus, Son of the Divine Augustus." Surely it must have galled faithful Jews to have to carry such a blasphemous statement around with them! We can almost imagine Jesus smiling slightly as he looked at the coin; the true "Son of

> Imagine the true "Son of the Divine" looking at the picture of this second-tier emperor.

the Divine" looking at the picture of this second-tier (in cosmic terms) emperor who liked to pretend that he was the son of a god! By all means give this little pretend god his shiny coin; but, to be clear, that is the extent of the honor that he is due. As Bock puts it,

> "affirms that Caesar has a domain that should be served and that God has a sphere where he should be honored ... Jesus' work for God does not challenge, but rather transcends, Rome."
> (*Luke 9:51 – 24:53*, page 1615)

Jesus has answered the spies' question, but what he says at the end of **verse 25** reframes it and takes the spring out of their trap (**v 26**):

not only must they give back to Caesar the things that belong to him, but they must give back to God what is God's. That is to say, if it is appropriate to give Caesar the things that bear his image, then it is only appropriate to give to God those things that bear his image. And what are those things? Everything. All of humanity bears God's image; everything comes from him and ultimately belongs to him. If Caesar deserves his coin, God deserves all that humanity has and is. The spies have come to play games and set political traps; Jesus tells them to give their lives to God.

These instructions are good news for us. Then, as now, rulers and governments are prone to set themselves up as would-be gods and saviors, and those under their authority are tempted to invest their hope in them. But no Caesar can save us, and we are free from having to give them more than what they are owed—namely, respect and conditional obedience. God has made us in his image, and so only he deserves (and can justly command) our ultimate love and allegiance. The One who has given us all we have is the one to whom we are to give our all.

The story of the poor widow giving her gift in the temple (**21:1-4**) serves as a perfect example of this radical giving to God. The woman was a poor widow (**v 2**), and her two copper coins seemed like an insignificant offering, especially when compared to the gifts that the wealthy were bringing into the temple treasury (**v 1**). But her gift was actually accounted as "more than all the others" (**v 3**) because instead of giving out of her excess and wealth, she gave (literally in the Greek) "all her life." She had nothing else; this gift represented her all. Caesar can have his tax payment; God wants us to dedicate our entire lives and all that we have to him.

Jesus warned his followers about the "teachers of the law" who, in contrast to the humble self-giving of the widow, sought glory and honor for themselves in all that they did (**20:45-46**). In fact, they preyed upon people like the poor widow, growing rich from the sacrificial giving of people like her—and Jesus promises that even though they seemed to prosper in this life, in the life to come they "will be punished most severely" (**v 47**). Then, as now, God's people must be on guard against those who see their supposed service to God as a way to wealth and the praise of men.

The Next Battleground: Resurrection

In **20:27**, Jesus is approached by some of the members of the Sadducees. This is the first time that Luke has mentioned this small sect of Jewish leaders. The Sadducees were the political and theological rivals of the Pharisees, which explains the positive reaction by the "teachers of the law" when Jesus flummoxes his questioners (**v 39**).

Theologically, the Sadducees were something like **rationalists**; they did not believe in the resurrection of the dead (**v 27**), claiming that life after death was a tradition made up by the Pharisees rather than a doctrine taught by the Old Testament. To prove their point, they had imagined a scenario that made the whole idea of the resurrection seem ridiculous (**v 28-33**). You can well imagine that this was not the first time they had used this argument; perhaps many a Pharisee had been stumped by their question.

To understand the situation that they present to Jesus, you have to know about the custom of levirate marriage, where the brother of a man who had died with no children would marry his widow, take care of her, and give her children in the dead brother's name (**v 28**; see Deuteronomy 25:5). In the Sadducees' scenario, each of seven brothers marry a particularly unfortunate woman and die without producing a child (**v 29-31**). Finally, mercifully, the woman dies as well (**v 32**).

In **verse 33**, they lay out the challenge. If there is a resurrection of the dead (as the Pharisees teach and which the Sadducees deny), who will ultimately be the one who is married to the woman? It seems that to them, this is an open-and-shut case; they have demonstrated that the idea of life after death is absurd. If we were raised from the dead, how could we possibly untangle all of the things that happen during our lives and after our deaths? Obviously, Jesus cannot say that they are all going to be married to her.

Jesus is not stumped by their challenge in the least; instead he corrects the ways that they have misunderstood the Scriptures and the power of God (see Mark 12:24) to create a world that is more wonderful than anyone can comprehend. The critical flaw in the Sadducees' thinking is that they assume that life after death is just like life now. But Jesus says that it is not so. Marriage is an institution for "this age" alone (Luke **20:34**); and there will be no marriage for the "children of the resurrection" (**v 36**) in the "age to come" (**v 35**). Jesus does not say explicitly why this is, but it could be because there is no longer a need to replenish the population through procreation since people are like the angels in that they "can no longer die."

That may seem discouraging to those who are enjoying (or hope to someday enjoy) the state of marriage in this life. But Scripture does indicate that we will know our loved ones in eternity, and surely the happiness and love of close relationships in heaven will be more rather than less than it is here on earth because heaven will be a place of perfect joy. God's power is such that he is able to create a world of greater joy, friendship and love in the life to come. In fact, the marriages that we enjoy here on earth are meant to give us a picture and foretaste of the far greater reality of the union with Christ that we will enjoy in eternity (Ephesians 5:31-32; Revelation 19:6-9). Human marriage, great though it is, is merely a preview; once the reality has come, it will no longer be necessary, and (strange as this may seem now) it will not be missed.

Jesus' ultimate point in saying these things is not to teach us about marriage or the nature of the eternal state, but rather, to dismiss the Sadducees' question and press on them the reality of the future resurrection. In Luke **20:36-38**, Jesus shows them that if they knew their Bibles, they would have already figured out that there was a resurrection of the dead. He reminds them of a statement that God made to Moses from the burning bush (found in Exodus 3:6), where he calls himself the God of Abraham, Isaac, and Jacob, all of whom had died long ago. If they were dead and their souls were gone, it stands to reason that God would not be their God anymore, at least not in the present tense. He would have to say to Moses that he *was* the God of Abraham, Isaac, and Jacob. Since God told Moses that he *is* the God of the patriarchs, they must still exist and death cannot be the final word for them. As Jesus summarizes it in Luke **20:38**, to God all are alive.

The reality of our future bodily resurrection is not merely some point of doctrine to be affirmed; it is a certainty that ought to control our lives in the here and now. The reason that we are able to follow the poor widow in giving our lives away in radical ways in the here and now is that we are certain that there will be an age to come when we will receive abundantly more than we could ever give away (remember 18:29-30; see Hebrews 11:8-10, 24-26). The hope of life after death means that we are not reduced to pursuing our best life now, a prospect almost as **existentially** depressing as it is theologically inaccurate.

Lord and Son?

At this point no one wants to ask Jesus any more questions (Luke **20:40**), and understandably so! And so instead Jesus asks them a question. Everyone listening to him would have believed that the Old Testament contained a promise that God would send the Messiah from the line and family of the great King David (**v 41**; see notes on Luke 9:20 in *Luke 1–12 For You,* pages 125-126). In light of that fact, Jesus asks them to explain a portion of Psalm 110 (quoted in Luke **20:42-43**), particularly the fact that in the psalm David calls this coming Messiah "my Lord." That is remarkable because David is talking about his descendant. A child might be taught to speak respectfully to his father (in parts of the United States, it is traditional for children to address their fathers as "Sir"), but fathers do not speak with that formal respect to their children. In Psalm 110, we would expect that David would call his descendant "son," not "Lord."

So Jesus asks them to explain how this coming Messiah can possibly be both David's son and also David's Lord (Luke **20:44**). The only possible answer is that the Messiah must be both David's son, and God's

Son—God's Son (and thus David's Lord) born into the great king's line. Though the conclusion is left unstated, the point is obvious: Jesus is the only one who makes sense of all the data. Because he is God's Son born into David's line, David's son and also David's Lord, he can secure our eternal life. He can promise us life in the age to come, which makes giving up everything that we have now worthwhile.

The posture of the religious leaders toward Jesus are in sharp contrast with that of Bartimaeus and Zacchaeus in the previous portion of this Gospel (Luke 18:35 – 19:10). Whereas they greeted Jesus with great joy and total devotion, the scribes and chief priests are only interested in playing games and trying to poke holes in Jesus' teaching. Instead of embracing the good news of the kingdom and acknowledging David's Lord as their Lord, they turn their backs to Jesus and miss out on the joy of discipleship. The same choice lies before us today—to obey Jesus' teaching gladly and find joy and blessing in it, or be so busy trying to find loopholes in his claims and commands that we miss out on the joy of simply trusting him and following them.

Questions for reflection

1. How do Jesus' words about Caesar and God help you to know how to respond to and think of the government of your country?

2. Why is it wonderful that the Lord of all creation takes time to notice, and to praise, a widow's small offering? What act of service does it encourage you to begin, or continue in, today?

3. How are you currently experiencing the blessing that comes from wholehearted, joyful obedience to Jesus' teaching?

9. THAT YOU MAY BE ABLE TO STAND

In the days before his crucifixion, Jesus spent his days teaching in the temple and spent the nights on the nearby Mount of Olives (**v 37-38**). Luke's account of Jesus' teaching in the temple began in 19:45, and chapter 21 marks the conclusion of his public ministry. It is a harrowing chapter, with predictions of destruction that alternate between the near horizon and things that will happen in the future.

The Temple's Demolition Date

The temple in Jesus' day was a spectacular architectural achievement, with massive stones, lavish furnishings, and a perimeter measuring almost a mile long. It was a monument to all of the strength and power and beauty and achievement that mankind could muster, and some of Jesus' disciples were remarking about how impressive it was (**21:5**). In light of the temple's splendor, Jesus' prediction in **verse 6** that it would one day be utterly destroyed was particularly shocking.

The disciples, perhaps chastened by watching Jesus dismantle both the scribes and the Sadducees in the previous conversations (see 20:40) do not dare to contradict Jesus' prediction, but instead they accept what he says as true and they ask the logical next question: when is all this going to happen (**21:7**)? What follows is an answer to their question, but also a lot more. Jesus launches off from this question and moves on to talk about a host of things that are going to happen in the future.

The challenge for interpreters is that Jesus alternates comfortably between the near horizon (the upcoming destruction of Jerusalem in

AD 70) and the distant horizon (his triumphant return and the end of the world as we know it). It is that alternation that seems to cause most of the confusion when people read these verses, but keeping it in mind will solve a lot of the passage's difficulties. We are positioned in history between the events that Jesus describes in this chapter; we can look back to the way that the Romans obliterated the temple, but we also look forward to the day when Jesus will return.

A Non-Answer Answer

Jesus' answer to their question does not actually provide the information they requested about the timing of the temple's demolition and the signs that will indicate that it is about to take place. Instead, he endeavors to prepare them for the events that will lead up to and surround the coming cataclysm. Jesus' commands come in the form of four "do not" statements.

In **verse 8**, he tells them not to be deceived, because many will come in Jesus' name claiming (literally) "I am" (see Exodus 3:14 and Luke 22:70) and that "the time is near." Jesus' words are borne out by history, as several messianic pretenders rose up in the years leading up to the destruction of the city. It is easy to understand how followers of Christ, anxious for his return and frightened by the looming specter of Roman military action, might be susceptible to a **charismatic** imposter claiming to be Jesus. But as the description in **21:27** indicates, when Jesus returns, there will be no ambiguity or wondering about whether it is truly he. If someone tries to convince you that he or she is Jesus, you can be sure that he or she is not. Jesus bluntly gives his second prohibition: "Do not follow them" (**v 8**).

The third "do not" statement comes in **verse 9**: "Do not be frightened" about reports of wars and uprisings. The time leading up to AD 70 would be marked by war (**v 10**), earthquakes, famines and pestilences, and terrifying signs in the heavens (**v 11**), all of which took place. As if that were not enough, Jesus warned them that before any of those terrible things would take place, the disciples would be delivered up. That phrase has the sense of being betrayed, perhaps by family or friends (which is confirmed in **verse 16**). They would be handed over to the synagogues and prisons, both the religious and civil authorities, all the way up the ladder to governors and kings (**v 12**). Luke's second volume in his history, the book of Acts, serves as a commentary on these verses, for this is exactly what happened to the disciples (see Acts 5:17-18; 12:1-3).

But while these are fearful events (Luke **21:11**), Jesus' purpose in forewarning the disciples is not to encourage the disciples to wildly speculate about the end times. Instead, he wants the disciples to be reassured by them. In fact, the trouble is not to be understood as a disaster, but a God-ordained opportunity to bear witness to him (**v 13**). In those moments the disciples are not to worry about their defense strategy (the fourth "do not" in this passage, **v 14**), because Jesus himself (the Greek word order is emphatic) promises to give them "words and wisdom" in that moment, which cannot be contradicted (**v 15**; see Acts 4:13-14). As we have already seen, Jesus is the very best person to have on your side if you are involved in a verbal altercation (Luke 20:26, 40).

The great news is that we can have this same confidence whenever we have an opportunity to testify to others about Jesus. Many a Christian has had the experience of being in a situation that was overwhelming and intimidating until God provided just the right words at just the right moment. You are not required to be the cleverest or most articulate and educated person. When God puts you in a situation to testify about him, you are called to be faithful—and you can be confident that he will help you and that Jesus really is enough.

> You are not required to be the cleverest or most articulate person. You are called to be faithful.

This does not mean, of course, that everyone you speak to will be convinced by the truth of the Christian message (though some will be!). In fact, Jesus promises his disciples that they will be betrayed, hated, and even put to death for his sake (**21:16-17**). But even in all of that, "not a hair of your head will perish" (**v 18**). In light of **verse 16**, this statement obviously cannot mean that believers will never be harmed physically. Instead, we should understand that Jesus is promising his people a far more important kind of protection (12:4-5)—the Lord's watch over their souls. The loss of one's life here on earth is relatively insignificant in light of eternity (9:24). By enduring hardship and by persevering through times of persecution, the disciples put themselves in the hands of God who will save their souls to eternal life. They are not commanded to do what they cannot do (save their physical lives), but by God's help they can stand firm faithfully to the end (**21:19**) and so be saved.

Jesus' predictions here were not only realized in the experience of the early church, where many were persecuted and martyred for their faith, but have also been realized in Christians in every age since that time. To follow Christ is to be an exile and a sojourner (1 Peter 2:11) in a world that frequently opposes believers with violence and persecution (2 Timothy 3:12). In the end, we can never be sure what part our individual lives play in the big picture of God's plan. It was persecution that forced the church to take the gospel to the entire world as God's people fled for their lives (Acts 8:1, 4).

It may be that God's plan for your life is for you to glorify him by running a relatively smooth course. But it may also be that God's plan for your life is for you to magnify him in your suffering. Or it may be a mixture of both. But either way, in these verses Jesus was utterly certain of God's sovereignty. What he told his disciples about their future had a remarkable correspondence to what actually happened in life. And the only way he could make such predictions that was because he knew what his Father had ordained to happen. These words do not amount to Jesus' best guess about the future; he is not reading the tea leaves or judging the way the wind blows. Instead, he is telling us what God will sovereignly bring to pass. And while that will include suffering for many of his followers, it will result in their ultimate salvation and the spread of his kingdom.

This is a good truth to have in place before suffering comes into your life. Get it firmly established in your mind now, so that when you are faced with trouble or the threat of trouble, you will be ready to respond with faith and confidence in God. The two things that are promised in this passage are future suffering and future triumph.

The End is Coming

Jesus moves on in Luke **21:20-24** to give his disciples more details on the topic of the coming demolition of Jerusalem (see 19:43-44). They had asked about the timing and indicators of when these things would take place (**21:7**), and now Jesus gives them some specific details. When they see Jerusalem surrounded by foreign armies, at that point they will know that "its **desolation** is near" (**v 20**). In fact, in AD 66 a revolt led by Jewish **zealots** led to a final war with the Romans, and by AD 70 the city had fallen and the people were either killed or taken off as prisoners (**v 24**).

Jesus' instructions are a remarkably practical field guide to surviving a foreign invasion: when the city is surrounded, those in the city must get out; those in the country should not make the mistake of fleeing into the city for protection, but rather, all the people of the region should flee to the relative safety of the mountains (**v 21**). The fate of those who cannot escape will be genuinely terrible, and Jesus expresses special concern for those who will have to suffer the extra stress and fear of trying to deal with those circumstances while pregnant or having responsibility for small children (**v 23**). We must not make the mistake of thinking that Jesus is vengefully delighting in the suffering that is coming to his enemies (remember his weeping over the city in 19:41, and see Lamentations 3:33).

But while Jesus does not take sadistic delight in these realities, it is still clear that they are realities ordained by God and sent in accordance with his sovereign will. The demolition of the city will be "the time of punishment" for its inhabitants' failure to acknowledge the Messiah that God had sent to them (Luke **21:22**; see 19:43-44). Just as the owner of the vineyard was completely justified in destroying the wicked tenants who had killed his son, so the Lord was only doing what was right when he sent the Roman armies into Jerusalem as a punishment for the people there.

All of this would be "in fulfillment of all that has been written" (Luke **21:22**), in that the Old Testament prophets repeatedly warned about the dangers of being unfaithful to the Lord. Significantly, Jesus' public ministry began with a proclamation that his acts of miraculous mercy were a fulfillment of the Scriptures (4:21). Now, in his final public discourse, he declares that the Scriptures will also be fulfilled when God's terrible judgment falls on Jerusalem.

These verses give us a window into a "tension" in the Bible's revelation of God's character that we must acknowledge. I hesitate to describe it in that way, for any sense of tension (or even worse, inconsistency) in the character of God is only a perceived tension; it must be a function of our lack of perfection and understanding. But, in any event, what we see in these verses is that God is both compassionate and just. He is patient and merciful, warning people to flee from the destruction that is coming. Even Jesus mentioning that the city would be trampled "until the times of the Gentiles are fulfilled" (**21:24**) indicates that God will use these events to further his saving mission to the non-Jewish nations, after which time there will be a renewal of Israel's spiritual fortunes (see Romans 11:25).

But God's mercy does not mean that he will delay forever in giving people the justice that they deserve for their sins (see Exodus 34:6-7). We cannot side with the "hellfire and brimstone" preachers who make God out to be a bloodthirsty monster bent on revenge, but neither can we side with the mealy-mouthed preachers who cannot imagine that God will one day hold people accountable for their sins. In fact, God is

far better than either of those one-sided caricatures c₂
both perfectly loving and perfectly just.

Questions for reflection

1. What are the institutions or cultural assumptions that seem im-
    movable and permanent to you? What do verses 5-6 say to this?

2. How would a disciple of Jesus in AD 70 felt to have read or heard
    these words from Luke's Gospel, do you think? What would it tell
    them about Jesus, and their decision to follow him?

3. Are you most concerned to protect the spiritual hairs on your
    head or the physical ones?

Future De-Creation

In Luke **21:25-28**, Jesus shifts to describe not the fall of Jerusalem in AD 70, but his own return from heaven. Jesus will be crucified, he will rise from the dead and ascend into heaven for an extended interval, and then he will return to finally and completely establish his kingdom with his people. The signs that will accompany his return are given without much detail of the specifics of what to expect—signs in the heavenly bodies, nations in anguish over the roaring and tossing of the sea, heavenly bodies being shaken. Whatever these signs look like, they will be so frightening that people will faint just from the terror that accompanies them (**v 26**).

What Jesus is describing here is nothing less than God de-creating the world. At creation, God calmed the chaos and divided up the waters. He created light, the sun and the moon, and put the stars in the heavens. And so Jesus seems to be casting his return in terms of a picture of God rolling back his creation, undoing this world in preparation for a new one. God will de-create this world because the Son of Man is coming back in glory (**v 27**).

These verses have been fertile soil in which all kinds of speculations and controversies have grown, but Jesus' intent seems to be to prepare and encourage his followers for that day. They will suffer persecutions and hardships at the hands of their fellow men (v 16), but the day of Jesus' return will be the arrival of their final redemption (**v 28**). The return of Christ will be terrifying to his enemies; Jerusalem's fall to Rome was just a small foretaste of what that final day will be like. But for Jesus's people, it will be a time of hope and promise.

Because there has been so much **spurious** teaching floating around regarding the return of Christ, many Christians are confused by and wary of the topic. But if you are a follower of Jesus, you should live with a sense of anticipation and longing for the return of Christ. In these verses Jesus holds out his return as the day of the redemption of his people. The return of Christ is not an event unrelated to the cross and resurrection of Jesus, but one wrapped up in the gospel message. As Edwards writes of the equivalent passage in Mark's Gospel (Mark 13:5-31):

> "The grand finale of the gospel preached by Jesus is that there is a sure hope for the future. It is grounded not in history or logic or intuition, but in the word of Jesus, in the **asseveration** that 'in those days' humanity will no longer usurp history but relinquish it to its Lord and Maker, who will return in glory and justice to condemn evil, end suffering, and gather his own to himself."
>
> (*The Gospel According to Mark*, page 402)

The return of Christ is then the grand finale of the gospel. On the cross Jesus purchased our redemption; when he returns he will consummate it.

Another Parable, Another Fig Tree

There is debate among scholars about whether Luke **21:29-32** should be understood to refer to the destruction of Jerusalem in AD 70 (**v 20-24**) or the ultimate return of the Son of Man to consummate his kingdom (**v 25-28**). The latter option has the advantage of immediately preceding the verses in question, but the former is probably the proper interpretation both because in **verse 32** Jesus seems to be looking for a specific reaction from the people immediately in front of him (none of whom would live to see his return in glory) and also because the Greek phrase for "these things" in both Luke's and Mark's accounts of these matters normally refers to the fall of Jerusalem (see 21:7, 9 and Mark 13:4)—so it is likely that in Luke **21:31** "these things" is also pointing us to AD 70.

In Luke **21:29**, Jesus points to a fig tree and draws a spiritual lesson from it (Luke labels the teaching a parable, even though it lacks that plot that we normally expect from the **genre**). The lesson is not bound up in the fig tree in particular, for it can be learned from observing "the fig tree and all the trees" (**v 29**). Like most trees, the fig tree sheds its leaves in winter and then regrows them once the cold weather has passed and warm weather is imminent. In that sense, its leaves serve as a sign of what is about to happen; when you see the fig tree sprouting leaves, "you can see for yourselves and know that summer is near" (**v 30**). In the same way, when the disciples saw the events described in verses 20-24 coming to pass, they would know that the destruction of Jerusalem, a key precursor to the return of Christ, was about to happen. In that sense "the kingdom of God is near" (**v 31**).

This passage presents interpretive challenges, but the end of the matter is that we should have great confidence in the fact that the return of Christ is a future certainty. We need not worry about the destruction of Jerusalem in AD 70, except to the extent that it serves as a reminder of God's commitment to carry out the judgment that he threatens. But we do live at a point in history where our eyes should be set forward to the day when the Son of Man comes with power and glory.

> The truth Jesus speaks will last far beyond the circumstances of our daily lives.

Jesus' declaration that his words will never pass away (**v 33**) reminds us that his authority is beyond our comprehension, and the truth that he speaks will last far beyond the circumstances of our daily lives that so consume us. We must have confidence in the words of Jesus, or else we will lack the faith to live now in light of his stated intention to return. We need not obsess over signs of Jesus' coming hidden in the news reports of the day; none of the signs that Jesus mentions in this passage seem very subtle or easily missed. The key will be in understanding the remarkable signs that everyone else sees as well. Jesus wants us to be prepared and to have understanding.

How Then Shall We Live?

We should understand Jesus' intent in this teaching as preparing his disciples for the destruction of Jerusalem. They needed to be on watch, praying for the strength and wisdom to endure "all that is about to happen": both the coming persecution (v 12-19) and the destruction of the city (v 20-24). If they stood firm (v 19), they would be able to stand before the Son of Man on that last day.

But Jesus is also preparing us for his return in glory. It is an event that will affect every person on earth (**v 35**) and it will come "suddenly like a trap" (**v 34**; see 12:40); thus it is incumbent upon followers of Christ to live each day in light of the approach of those days (see 12:35-40). We also need to be watchful and devoted to prayer so that we can endure whatever persecution and hardships the Lord might see fit for us to endure as his followers.

But perhaps the greatest threat to our spiritual wellbeing is not the threat of widespread anti-Christian violence or personal persecution, but the daily temptations and distractions that can easily take root once we stop living in light of Christ's imminent return in glory. The temptation as we wait for that final day is to begin to live as if Jesus is not actually coming back: to settle in here, to make this life our ultimate home, and to begin to live for it alone.

If you do settle in that way, then the "anxieties of life" (**21:34**; see 8:14) will begin to take on supreme importance to you. You will begin to invest all of your energy, your love, and your passion in the things of this life. You will give everything that you have to looking attractive, having a great job, making enough money, finding the perfect spouse, and raising exceptional children. All of those things can feel much more real and certain than the return of Christ. After all, our calendars and bank balances are daily issues that we can see and must deal with, but we have never once experienced the return of the Son of Man in glory. But if we are not careful, and we allow these other things in our lives to occupy and distract our hearts, even if they are ostensibly "good", they will become spiritually malignant.

This applies even more to the sinful pleasures that the world offers. Jesus warns against "drunkenness" and "carousing" (the Greek word has the sense of the throbbing headache that arrives in the wake of a night of heavy drinking). These are characteristic sins of someone who has embraced the world's pleasures wholeheartedly. These are the kinds of things that someone engages in when they are trying to find all of their meaning and joy here and now. No one ever looked at pornography, flirted with someone who was not their spouse, or ran up credit-card debts on things they cannot afford with their hearts set expectantly on the reality that Jesus would return. It would be wise for every Christian to examine his or her life for those things that will seem foolish and regrettable on that last day.

Followers of Jesus should be different from the people of the world, who care not one whit for the reality of Christ's return. We should "watch and pray" that we would be able to withstand the corroding influences of living in a world that is constantly developing new and more compelling ways to seek all of our joy and pleasure in the here and now. We are to be watchful, like stewards expecting their master to return any day, knowing that we will give an account to him, and that he comes bearing blessing and reward for those who are faithful. And we must pray, because this is not an easy task that we can accomplish in our own strength. The very fact that Jesus commands his followers to be watchful indicates that this is not the direction in which the current of life's river will take us.

Before we leave this passage, it is worth noting how many commands it contains for us. We may feel somewhat helpless in light of the events that will lead up to the end times, but there is plenty for us to do. Believers must "watch out" (v 8), "make up your mind" (v 14), "stand firm" (v 19), and "be careful" (**v 34**). We are to "be always on the watch, and pray" so that we will be "able to stand before the Son of Man" (**v 36**). Living in light of Christ's return is a way of life that requires diligence, effort, and God's help; no one will be found accidentally faithful on that last day. This is a complex chapter, with a very simple application: be careful and watchful and deliberate and prayerful about standing firm and looking forward today, so you will be able to stand on the last day.

Questions for reflection

1. How can you make sure you lift your head up and look forward toward Christ's coming?

2. What aspect of worldly pleasure or anxiety do you need to "be careful" of, because it could cause you to stop watching for Jesus to come?

3. Do you pray for perseverance in facing hardship and suffering? Or do you assume hardship will not come to you, or that you will be able to face it in your own strength?

10. THE NIGHT OF TRIALS

Jesus' popularity with the crowds had made it virtually impossible for the religious leaders to lay hands on him (**22:2**; see Luke 20:19) and the approach of the **Passover** and the accompanying **Feast of Unleavened Bread** (**22:1, 7**) made it even more so. Since much of his ministry was spent in Galilee, Jesus was understandably quite popular with the crowds of pilgrims from that region who were thronging into the city for the celebration. If the chief priests and the teachers of the law wanted to arrest Jesus "when no crowd was present" (**v 6**), they would need help from someone on the inside of Jesus' circle of disciples.

The Betrayal Begins

That help arrived in the form of Judas Iscariot, one of the twelve disciples (see 6:16). He pursued the leaders about how he might betray Jesus to them (**22:4**), his betrayal ultimately taking the form of leading them to a place where they could find Jesus when the crowds were not around (v 47). We are not told exactly why Judas did what he did, though some have speculated that he was frustrated by Jesus' unwillingness to seize political power and overthrow Rome.

That is a possible explanation, but in the end all that the Bible tells us is that Judas never really believed in Jesus (see John 6:64, 70; 12:4-6). Whatever his personal motivations (beyond the obvious factor of greed, Luke **22:5**), Luke does tell us that Judas was acting under the influence of Satan, who had entered into him (**v 3**). This does not in any way excuse Judas' actions, as **verses 21-22** make clear; even though it was ordained that the Son of Man would go to the cross, Judas would be condemned for his act of betrayal.

We have been prepared for this re-entrance of the evil one ever since chapter 4, where Satan skulked away from his confrontation with Jesus in the wilderness "until an opportune time" (4:13—see the echo in the description of Judas in **22:6**). That opportune time had now come, and Satan came alongside Judas and the leaders of Israel as a co-conspirator.

Do not miss the drama of the moment; since the very beginning, the devil had been trying desperately to thwart God's plan to bless his people (see Genesis 3:1-5), and this was his big chance. If he could kill the one who was supposed to deliver God's people, then, he believed, they would not be saved. This is why, when his enemies finally find him and arrest him, Jesus tells them that, "This is your hour—when darkness reigns" (Luke 22:53).

The Last Supper

While Judas waited for an opportunity to betray his master, the band of disciples had to undertake preparations for the Passover celebration. To that end Jesus sent Peter and John, two of his most trusted disciples, to make the necessary arrangements (**v 8-9**), and the events unfolded in a way that calls to mind the way in which the colt had been procured for Jesus' entry into the city (19:29-34). They would be met by "a man carrying a jar of water" (**22:10**), which would have attracted the disciple's attention, as in those days that was a task normally carried out by women. The man with the water jar would lead the disciples to a residence where the master would show them the place to prepare the meal (**v 10-12**). Some have speculated that Jesus had made these arrangements in advance and had kept them from the disciples in order to prevent Judas from betraying him before he could celebrate the Passover with the disciples, something he longed to do before his suffering (**v 15**). But whatever the purpose of the unusual instructions, the disciples "found things just as Jesus had told them" (**v 13**) and there the group was able to recline at the table together (**v 14**).

Luke's account of the meal itself is marked by a sense that something is coming to an end. Jesus acknowledges that he will not eat this meal or drink the cup again until they find their fulfillment in the kingdom of God (**v 16-18**) at the **consummation** of all things (Revelation 19:9). But there is also a sense in which something is beginning in this meal. Jesus tells the disciples that they should "do this" in remembrance of him (Luke **22:19**). Jesus anticipated that there would be an extended period of time in which the disciples would use this meal not to remember the Passover, but to remember him.

Jesus is instituting a new meal for his people to observe as they remember their salvation, one that we continue until this day in our Lord's Supper celebration. Jesus is declaring that his upcoming death is the greater, final act of salvation by God. The exodus from Egypt was the defining act of salvation under the old **covenant**, and the Passover was the way God's people remembered it. But now God's people remember the greater sacrifice of the true Passover lamb (see 1 Corinthians 5:7) and the arrival of a new covenant (Luke **22:20**; see Jeremiah 31:31) by celebrating the Lord's Supper together in churches.

The Passover meal involved four cups of wine and the eating of unleavened bread. Jesus used the ceremonial breaking of the bread to symbolize the way that his body would be "given" on the cross (**v 19**). The cup of dark red wine was a picture of the way that his blood would be "poured out" for them (**v 20**). Jesus was about to stand in as the true Passover lamb, who would be sacrificed for the sins of his people.

Just as the blood of the slaughtered lamb in the exodus offered protection from the plague on the firstborn, so now the blood of Jesus shelters his people from the awful and fearsome consequences of their sin. God's judgment does not fall on the one who is protected by the "blood of the Lamb" (Revelation 7:14-15). The millions of

Passover lambs sacrificed over the years, including those sacrificed on that particular day (Luke **22:1, 7**), were all meant to point forward to the one real Passover lamb, who would shed his blood to protect his people from judgment.

> Guilty, vile, and helpless we,
> Spotless Lamb of God was he,
> "Full atonement!" Can it be?
> Hallelujah! What a Savior!
>
> ("Man of Sorrows, What a Name!" by Philip P. Bliss)

The (Not So) Great Debate

In a culture that prized hospitality, the idea of betraying someone with whom you had shared table fellowship was particularly repugnant (see David's lament in Psalm 41:9). Thus Jesus' statement in Luke **22:21-22** doubtlessly shocked the little band of disciples, and they began wondering to whom Jesus was referring (**v 23**). That act of looking inwards seemed to have given rise to the terrible debate that followed; having wondered which of them was the very worst (and thus would betray their master), they moved on to argue over which of them was the greatest (**v 24**).

It is easy to condemn the disciples for their obsession with their own personal greatness. But we see the same impulse in our own lives—from parents who find their meaning in their children's accomplishments to the person who is obsessed with outperforming his or her peers at work, we long to be recognized as extraordinary. If we are honest, most of us want personal glory in the same way that the disciples did; we are simply too proud(!) to argue about it out loud with others.

Now, we would understand if Jesus had flipped over the table in righteous indignation at this point; there could not be a more inappropriate moment to talk about personal glory. But instead, Jesus simply reminds them that these kinds of things are what motivate the leaders of the outside world (**v 25**). His followers, however, "are not to be like that" (**v 26**). What a difference it would make if Christians today simply took that one principle to heart! Being a follower of Jesus means that we ought to find places where our values and love are in stark contradiction to those of the world around us.

The disciples' craving for personal glory was perhaps normal, but they were pursuing it the wrong way. In the economy of Christ's kingdom, great people act as if they are the person who is the youngest (and thus, least worthy of honor); the one who rules should be like the one who waits tables (**v 26**). The disciples had been faithful in standing by Jesus in his trials (**v 28**, though compare the ominous note sounded in **v 31-32**), and so just as the Father had conferred a kingdom on the Son of Man (**v 29**; see Daniel 7:13-14), so Jesus was conferring a kingdom upon them so that they could exercise authority in his eternal kingdom (Luke **22:30**).

> The one who rules should be like the one who waits tables.

Perhaps the most compelling reason for Christians to be humble is located in Jesus' comments in **verse 27**. If a server is not greater than the person he waits upon at the table, then (by implication) the disciples are not greater than Jesus their master. And if Jesus' conduct "among" them has been "as one who serves," how can his disciples possibly be obsessed with whether or not they appear great to others? Christians in positions of leadership, whether in the home, the church, or the workplace, must be marked by the same servant's mindset that Jesus demonstrated (see Philippians 2:1-8).

Jesus' ultimate act of service was his death on the cross for sinners (see Mark 10:45), and that explains why humility must be right at the heart of our response to the gospel. As Jesus has repeatedly made clear, his salvation is reserved for those who know their desperate need for mercy (see Luke 18:9-17). And in fact, the crucifixion is a reminder that we are not inherently good and worthy of God's love.

Rather, our sin is such that the Son of God had to suffer that in order for us to be acceptable to God. If that is the case, there is really nothing about us worthy of exalting. The best way to kill pride in your heart is to contemplate the humility of Jesus, seen most clearly in his willingness to die for people like us (Philippians 2:3-8).

You're Going to Need a Sword

It is amazing that as he faced the horrors that awaited him in the coming 24 hours, Jesus still took time to care for and prepare his disciples. Turning to Peter as the leader of the disciples, Jesus warned him that Satan had "asked" (the Greek word has the sense of demanding presumptuously) to sift all of the disciples like wheat (the "you" in Luke **22:31** is plural). Wheat was sifted by shaking it violently in order to separate the good from the useless parts, and in a similar way the events of the coming days would be a terrible and revealing test for the small band of disciples.

Jesus, knowing full well that Peter would deny him three times in the coming hours (**v 34**), prayed that his faith would not fail and that he would not be destroyed in the process (**v 32**). Knowing full well that Peter would turn back, Jesus called him to the ministry of caring for the other disciples. Instead of hearing and heeding Jesus' warning, Peter responded with self-confident words (**v 33**). In the end, he would be imprisoned and even martyred for the sake of Christ, but at that moment he was not anywhere close to ready to fulfill his boast.

The other disciples would experience Satan's sifting as well, and so Jesus turned to instruct them next. He had sent them out twice previously without provisions (9:3 and 10:4), and they had lacked nothing (**22:35**). Going forward, however, everything would be different. Back in those earlier days, they did not need to bring provisions because Jesus' popularity translated into plenty of support, but now persecution and trouble would be the order of the day.

If there were any doubt about the severity of the coming trouble, Jesus' instruction to exchange one's cloak for a sword would lay it to rest (**v 36**). Whenever weapons are more important than clothing, difficult times are afoot. But in light of the overwhelming trajectory of Jesus' ministry (see 6:27-31; 9:52-56; 22:51), it is almost certainly best to understand that the sword in view here is, Edwards says:

> "[a] metaphor of admonition and preparedness, not a sanction to spread the gospel by violence."

> *(The Gospel According to Luke,* page 640)

If that is the case, then Jesus' statement in **verse 38** was not an affirmation that two swords would be sufficient for the upcoming situation (clearly they were not!), but rather, a way of telling them to drop the subject of swords altogether.

All of the trouble that is coming to the disciples will be as a result of their relationship to a master who is going to be rejected and disgraced. He is the one about whom Isaiah 53 was written, and so it must be that he will be "numbered with the transgressors" (**Luke 22:37**; see Isaiah 53:12). That prophecy will be fulfilled in just a few hours, as Jesus is crucified between two criminals. Jesus' followers, then as now, should not expect to be treated by the world with more honor and respect than their master was (John 15:20).

Questions for reflection

1. How have these verses caused you to love Jesus more?

2. Jesus knew his disciples would betray him, fail him, and deny him… yet he still walked toward the cross. How does knowing he knew these things increase our awe of his sacrifice?

3. Are there ways you expect or demand to be treated better than Jesus was by this world? What would change in your life and your joy if you did not expect this?

PART TWO

The Agony of the Son of God

After leaving the Passover meal, Jesus went with his disciples to the Mount of Olives (Luke **22:39**), a place he went to frequently. When he reached "the place" (identified by other Gospel writers as the Garden of Gethsemane—see Matthew 26:36), he twice instructed them that they should use the time to pray that they would not enter into temptation (Luke **22:40, 46**). But instead of praying they fell asleep, exhausted by their sorrow (**v 45**); it is clear that whatever Jesus was about to experience, he would go through it completely alone.

Jesus himself went a little way away to pray (**v 41**), but instead of finding comfort and peace in his communion with his heavenly Father, Jesus began to experience something terrible, so much so that an angel had to be sent to strengthen him (**v 43**). Luke tells us that he was in agony, experiencing such anguish that his sweat was like blood as he prayed even more earnestly (**v 44**). The picture painted for us is one of a person in total "system overload"; Jesus' physical body and human nature could barely endure what was happening.

What could possibly cause this kind of agony? Certainly it could not be the mere fear of pain or death. After all, Jesus had been speaking about his upcoming crucifixion for some time without any of this kind of anguish. But we see the reason in **verse 42**, where Jesus identified the source of his turmoil as "this cup." And in fact, Mark's and Matthew's Gospels tell us that Jesus cried out three separate times for relief from "this cup" (Matthew 26:39-44; Mark 14:35-39).

In the Old Testament, the prophets of Israel sometimes spoke of God's wrath and judgment against sin as a cup that the wicked were required to drink (see Isaiah 51:17 and Jeremiah 25:15-16 for two examples). The cup is symbolic, representing the fury, anger, and punishment of God. To put it simply, the cup that Jesus prays about is full of God's perfect and holy hatred for sin. And here on the Mount of Olives, Jesus begins to taste what is in that cup, unmingled and undiluted by God's mercy. He begins to experience what will be required of him on the cross if he is to save his people.

For those of us who have received forgiveness through Jesus' blood, we have here in the Garden of Gethsemane a beautiful picture of our Lord's love for us. We cannot imagine what it was like for Jesus to endure the cross. If just a taste, just the anticipation of that wrath, was enough to make Jesus fall to the ground and sweat drops of blood, how much worse was his actual experience at his crucifixion? But so great was Jesus' love for his Father and for us, he went willingly to the cross, knowing what he would experience there.

Jesus prayed that the cup might be removed from him (Luke **22:42**), and understandably so. If there were any other way for God's people to be saved, it had to be preferable to experiencing the wrath-filled cup. But ultimately, Jesus' highest priority was doing God's will, even if it cost him everything.

This brief but dramatic episode teaches us something important about what it means to be a follower of Jesus. His highest priority was the will of his heavenly Father, even when it was costly and dangerous. And so even as Jesus taught us to pray "your will be done" (Matthew 6:10), we must recognize that obedience to God's will may often be difficult and painful. It is not enough to merely pray that prayer, we must also be willing to obey and, if necessary, suffer the loss of our convenience, our reputation, even our lives.

Betrayed and Denied

When "a crowd" (Luke **22:47**) including "the chief priests, the officers of the temple guard, and the elders" (**v 52**) came up the mountainside with Judas at the head, his enemies finally had the opportunity they had sought for so long. Jesus' followers could see that his arrest was inevitable (**v 49**), and one disciple (identified as Peter in John 18:10) lashed out with a sword, cutting off the ear of the high priest's servant (Luke **22:50**). Jesus, in his final miracle before his death, healed the man's ear and rebuked his disciple (**v 51**). His

> Jesus' victory would not be won with swords and his kingdom would not be opened with violence.

victory would not be won with swords and his kingdom would not be opened with violence.

From this point on in Luke's narrative, Jesus will be in the custody of his enemies and on his way to the cross. And while he does not approve of violent resistance, that does not mean that he will go silently. Instead, he confronts Judas about his treachery—will he really betray the Son of Man with a kiss (**v 48**)? This is one last act of kindness by the Lord; surely the intention of his question was not to gain information but to give Judas one last opportunity to reconsider. He has no such tenderness toward the cowardly religious leaders, but instead he draws attention to the fact that they have come against him in the darkness with swords and clubs instead of choosing an honest, open confrontation in the temple courts (**v 52-53**).

After the arrest, the mob took Jesus away to be interrogated at the home of the high priest. Luke notes that Peter "followed at a distance" (**v 54**) and eventually sat down near a fire that had been lit in the courtyard (**v 55**), surely hoping that he would not be noticed. What follows are three acts of betrayal that, while not as malicious as that of Judas, were certainly every bit as shocking. First, when a servant girl recognized him as one of Jesus' compatriots, he denied even knowing him (**v 56-57**). Next, an unidentified person suggested that Peter was one of Jesus' disciples, but he denied it (**v 58**). An hour later yet another person, most likely identifying Peter as a Galilean by his accent, figured out that he was really one of Jesus' disciples, but Peter disavowed all knowledge of Jesus and his followers (**v 59-60**). It seems that it had finally sunk in for Peter: Jesus was really going to die; he really wasn't going to fight back. There would be no revolution, no glory, and no victory, so he might as well save his own skin.

Just in case he ever someday was tempted to think that he wasn't a liar and a coward, Peter could look back to this moment and remember the truth. For all his bluster about how he would die for Jesus (v 33), how he would never betray him or deny him, Peter totally crumpled in the face of a slave girl and two strangers. And so at the very moment of Peter's third denial, a rooster crowed (**v 60**), calling to mind Jesus' earlier prediction to that effect (**v 61**, see v 34). When Jesus turned and looked at Peter, Peter went out and wept bitterly (**v 62**) at his own weakness and sorrow over what was happening to Jesus.

Though it seems like merely a record of terrible failure, in fact the story of Peter's denial is good news for us. In the end Peter was restored, just as Jesus had predicted back in verse 32. And that restoration could only take place because Jesus willingly died for Peter's sin, including the sin of denying Jesus three times in his moment of greatest distress. And that means that there is forgiveness and hope for all of us who, like Peter, have ever found our courage and love lacking. If you have ever remained silent when you should have spoken up for Jesus, or if you have ever hidden what you really believe so that people will not reject you, then you are not so different from Peter. And so the great thing about Jesus is that his love covers even sins like these.

That truth should lead us to heartfelt repentance when we sin. That is the difference between Peter and Judas. Both sinned against their master in terrible ways, but Judas' remorse never led him back to Jesus. Peter on the other hand, repented and returned to being a disciple. Because Jesus died for his people's sins, there is mercy and forgiveness for everyone who falls and fails. When you sin, do not run from Jesus; run to him!

The Mockery of the Savior

The decision to arrest Jesus at night presented the religious leaders with a problem. Jewish law required that any capital charge be heard by an official meeting of the Sanhedrin, a group of 71 men that included respected leaders, teachers of the religious law, and prominent priests (Luke usually refers to this group as "the council"). The Jewish custom also required that such a meeting had to take place during daylight hours; we can easily understand why the law would forbid trials and judgments under the cover of darkness. Jesus' popularity with the crowds meant that there was pressure on his enemies to have him condemned to death before word spread that he had been arrested.

So when the leaders finally arrest Jesus, they face a conundrum. They've finally captured this guy that they've been trying to outfox for all this time, but they can't afford to sit on him for very long. The crowds seem to love Jesus, and the leaders don't dare wait and let the word get out that Jesus has been arrested. So they want to get his case wrapped up, so that Jesus can be condemned and put to death as soon as possible.

But in the meantime, the guards who were watching Jesus began to have a little fun with him. They beat Jesus (**v 63**—the Greek word that Luke uses seems to indicate that the beating went on for some period of time), mocked him, and hurled insults at him (**v 65**) as they struck him. Since Jesus had a reputation as a prophet, they also decided to put his skills to the test. They blindfolded him, punched him and taunted him, challenging him to guess who it was who hit him (**v 64**).

All of this was to fulfill the words of the prophets (see Isaiah 50:6 and 52:14). But it also means that we, as followers of Christ, will never endure any kind of suffering or humiliation that Jesus does not understand. When other people are unkind to us, when they abuse us (in small ways or in big ways), when we are mocked or shut out because we love Jesus, it can make us weary. It can tempt us to give up and wonder if God really cares. But you will not find him distant or unconcerned, but able to sympathize with all of your weakness and pain. This is why Hebrews 12:3 instructs us to look at Jesus and, "consider him who endured such opposition from sinners, so that you will not grow weary and lose heart."

The Trial of Jesus and of His Accusers

When the council can finally be convened at daybreak, Jesus is led before them to stand trial (Luke **22:66**). When they try to get him to go on the record as claiming to be the Messiah, Jesus refuses to answer directly, knowing that a conversation about the topic is wasted on those who have already made up their minds (**v 67-68**; see 20:8). What he says next, however, is even more shocking than a claim to be the Messiah. He is not only the Messiah, but he is the divine Son of Man from Daniel 7:13-14. After his crucifixion, resurrection, and ascension, he "will be seated at the right hand of the mighty God" (Luke **22:69**).

Claiming to be the Messiah was not technically blasphemy, but claiming to be the Son of God (if in fact you were not) most certainly was. The leaders understand the significance of what Jesus is saying, and they ask him to confirm that he believes himself to be the Son of God (**v 70**). Jesus' response is neither an open affirmation nor a flat denial: "You say that I am." We might see a similar expression in our idiom, "You said it; I didn't," where one wants to affirm a truth while making someone else responsible for saying it. The council's angry (and delighted?) response shows that they understand it that way (**v 71**). They finally have what they need to see Jesus executed.

There is, of course, a great irony in the fact that Jesus is standing trial before the religious leaders of the people. How far astray these leaders have gone that they have put the Son of Man on trial, that they dare to sit in judgment over him! And not only that, but they actually find him guilty of blasphemy, of lying about God!

But this miscarriage of justice is also a perfect picture of the humility and love of Jesus. How incredible that the Son of God, by whom all things were created, would stoop down to allow his creatures to treat him this way! In a sense, God condescends to allow each and every one of us to pass judgment on him. Of course, he is God (and Jesus is the Son of Man) whether or not we choose to acknowledge that reality. But God permits us to decide what we will make of his

Son Jesus: whether he is worthy of our exclusive love and worship and devotion as he claimed, or whether he is a blasphemer and a liar as his enemies believed. In that sense, every person who hears the message about Jesus must put themselves in the place of the religious leaders and decide what they believe him to be.

But don't be deceived by God's kindness. Jesus stands before these men absorbing their scorn and abuse, but he has promised to return, this time not to suffer but to execute terrible judgment on all those who have rejected him (17:26-30). Right now you have the life and breath to decide whether you will willingly worship God's Son or not. But know for sure that a day will come when:

"At the name of Jesus every knee [will] bow, in heaven and on earth and under the earth, and every tongue acknowledge that Jesus Christ is Lord, to the glory of God the Father."

(Philippians 2:10-11)

Questions for reflection

Right now, how will you...

1. acknowledge the awfulness, and weep at the reality of, your sin?

2. enjoy the knowledge that your Lord knows you completely, yet still loves you enough that he chose to die for you?

3. find comfort in your own difficulties from knowing that Jesus has faced worse, and yet remained truthful and loyal?

11. THREE CRIMINALS AND ONE KING

Luke's account of the events leading up to the crucifixion moves forward at a breakneck pace. Full of short vignettes and memorable interactions, chapter 23 shows humanity at its very worst—cowardice, duplicity, and hatred are the order of the day. But it is in the deepest darkness that we see the strength, love, and dignity of Jesus shine even more brightly.

He Claims to Be a King

Following the determination by the Sanhedrin that Jesus was guilty of blasphemy (22:71), the proceedings moved to Governor Pilate's headquarters (**23:1**). In order to have Jesus put to death, they had to overcome two related obstacles. First, Rome reserved the right to execute criminals and did not permit the Jewish authorities to put anyone to death (John 18:31). Second, and linked to that political reality, even if Jesus was guilty of blasphemy, the Roman authorities would not consider that to be a crime worthy of punishment. Rome cared not a whit for the religious scruples of other cultures, and so Jesus' enemies would have to accuse Jesus of a crime that Rome would find worthy of death.

To that end, the Sanhedrin lodges three charges against Jesus that might serve to get Pilate's interest (Luke **23:2**). First, they claim that Jesus has been "subverting our nation." The heart of the accusation is that Jesus is dangerous and might start a mob rebellion against Roman rule. Second, they claim that Jesus "opposes payment of taxes to Caesar." Certainly this would interest Pilate, even though it was manifestly false (see 20:20-26). The third charge, however, is both true, and explosive: Jesus, they tell Pilate, "claims to be Messiah, a king."

And it is that last charge that gets Pilate's interest. He turns his attention to Jesus and questions him directly as to whether he claims to be the king of the Jews (**23:3**). We can imagine that Jesus, standing there having been bound, blindfolded, and beaten, sleep-deprived and spit-covered, did not look particularly regal at that moment. And so perhaps Pilate's question should be understood sarcastically: "*You're the king of the Jews? You?!*"

Jesus' answer is reminiscent of his response to the Sanhedrin back in 22:70. He does not deny what is true, for he has just claimed to have received a kingdom from his Father (22:29). But neither does he engage in pointless banter with someone who is not really interested in God's truth. Jesus was most definitely not a king after the pattern of rulers like Pilate and Caesar. He had no interest in a political kingdom established through politics and force.

Pilate could sense quickly that Jesus presented no immediate threat to Rome's rule, and so he initially refused to take action against Jesus, finding "no basis for a charge" against him (**23:4**). But the Jewish leaders were not going to be dissuaded, and their next play was to accuse Jesus of being an agitator (**v 5**). Surely Pilate would take interest in someone who might destabilize the region and stir up mob violence. They overplayed their hand, however, and when they mentioned that Jesus began his ministry in the region of Galilee, Pilate saw a potential way out of the situation (**v 6-7**). Since Galilee fell under the authority of Herod Antipas and he happened to be in the city for the Passover, Pilate could send Jesus to him in what would seem like a gesture of respect (and was ultimately received as such, **v 12**) but would also allow Pilate to avoid responsibility for Jesus' fate.

Herod was "greatly pleased," for he had been wanting to see (and perhaps even kill—13:31) Jesus for "a long time" (**23:8**). In keeping with what we know about Herod, his interest in Jesus was not motivated by a sincere desire to understand the truth. Instead, he hoped to see a sign or have an interesting conversation (**v 8-9**), but Jesus would not answer him even as his enemies continued to accuse him "vehemently" (**v 10**).

There is a terrible irony in what happens next, when Herod and his soldiers mockingly dress Jesus up in an elegant robe of the sort that a king would wear (**v 11**). The idea that Jesus could be a king was ludicrous to them, but little did they know the truth—that he really was the long awaited king of the Jews. Jesus was the descendant of the great King David who would reign on his throne forever, just as God had promised to David in 2 Samuel 7 (Luke 1:32). What Pilate and Herod could not understand was that this king's kingdom was not coming through military might or political skill; he would come to his throne through a cross, a brutal instrument of execution. The mocking inscription above the cross (23:38) spoke the truth: *This is the King of the Jews.*

Herod and his men dressed Jesus in a royal robe as a mocking response to his claim to be a king. But when a Christian thinks about Jesus in that robe, enduring the taunts and ridicule of the soldiers, we see the proof that Jesus is the heroic king we've always wanted. He is worthy of all our allegiance and trust, both in the face of difficulties we face today and with our eternal destiny.

Give Us Barabbas

The verdict was in. Herod sent Jesus back (**v 11**) with a "not-guilty" verdict (**v 15**), which he gives and now Pilate adds his own vote to that same verdict (**v 14**) to the crowd that he has called together (**v 13**). It is important to remember that Pilate is absolutely convinced that Jesus is innocent; otherwise, nothing that follows will seem quite as horrible as it should. Repeatedly Pilate meets the bloodthirstiness of the crowd with a desire to release Jesus (**v 20**) and a reminder that Jesus has not actually committed any crimes (**v 22**). But Pilate is ultimately too much of a coward to do the right thing. He fears the crowds, and so he tries several times to appease them without having to actually put Jesus to death. In a kind of terrible **plea-bargain**, he offers to have the innocent man punished (**v 16** and **v 22**), but the crowds respond by shouting, "Away with this man!" (**v 18**).

Pilate's next move is to set Jesus free under the terms of an annual prisoner-release program (**v 17**—note that this verse includes an intro- duction to this idea, similar to ones in Matthew 27:15 and Mark 15:6, but it is not present in the best manuscripts of Luke 23 and should be understood as a later addition). Not much is known about Barabbas beyond the fact that he was in prison for insurrection and murder (Luke **23:19**), but we can assume that he was the worst prisoner on hand, for Pilate clearly wanted to give the crowd the worst option possible so that they would choose Jesus (see Matthew 27:21). But the crowd was unwilling, insisting that Jesus be done away with while Barabbas was released instead (Luke **23:18**).

By this point, Pilate was running out of options. He pressed again for Jesus' release (**v 20**), but the crowd become all the more enraged and demanded his crucifixion (**v 21**). He appealed to the crowd "a third time," pressing on them the reality of Jesus' innocence and of- fering once more to have him punished before releasing him (**v 22**). But the crowd "insistently demanded" that Jesus be crucified (**v 23**), and Pilate eventually caved in to their desires (**v 24**). Barabbas was released and Jesus was condemned (**v 25**).

Here is a dramatic picture of what Jesus was about to do for his people at the cross. Imagine what it would be like to be Barabbas on that day, sitting in a Roman jail awaiting the most gruesome death imaginable. On this fateful day you hear a mob outside; clearly some- thing is going on. Has word gotten out that today is your day, the day of your death? It sounds like it; you can hear the crowd screaming, "Crucify him! Crucify him!"

But when the guard comes to get you, instead of placing the cross on your back, he unlocks your shackles and sets you free. As you stand there, you watch another man stumble off under the weight of the cross—the very cross you had imagined would be yours. When you ask someone in the crowd what this man has done to deserve this fate, the answers are surprisingly vague. All you know is that you have been chosen for life and he has been chosen for death.

> As you stand there, you watch another man stumble off under the cross you had imagined would be yours.

Barabbas was a terribly guilty man; there is no doubt that he deserved the cross that waited for him. But what we see is that Jesus went off to die in his place. Barabbas, the guilty man, went free and Jesus, the innocent man, was treated like a criminal. Jesus bore the guilt and shame and curse and disgrace and death that Barabbas deserved, while Barabbas received the release, the freedom, and the life that Jesus deserved.

Barabbas walked out that day a free and innocent man as far as the law was concerned; Jesus was the condemned one. In the same way, you and I are sinners; we sit in a spiritual prison, bound helpless, awaiting the day when we get the just punishment that we deserve. But then Jesus has gone off to the cross in our place. He has got what we deserve; we get what he deserves.

Mob Rule, Then and Now

How do we account for the vitriol and hatred of the crowd? This was not the work of a few isolated agitators, for Luke tells us that the "whole crowd" (**v 18**), consisting of "the chief priests, the rulers, and the people" (**v 13**), were united in calling for Jesus to be taken away. This was a universal, unanimous verdict of people from every walk of life and social class (see Peter's words to the people of Jerusalem in Acts 3:13-15).

If Barabbas is a picture of the individual, condemned for his sins and in need of a substitute to bear his punishment, perhaps we are meant to see in the crowd the natural enmity that all people have toward God. When it came down to a choice, these people preferred to have a murderer live among them rather than the Son of God. Rightly has the pastor and theologian R.C. Sproul called this scene outside of Pilate's hall, "God in the Hands of Angry Sinners" (*The Holiness of God,* page 180).

Sinful human beings simply cannot be neutral toward a holy God. We are rebels against him and he is a threat to our way of life. He stands between us and our passionate commitment to live our lives in exactly the way that we wish. And so when God came in human flesh, the only options open to humanity were to worship him as Lord or kill him as an enemy.

Do not be overly confident that you would have acted differently if you had been present in that crowd. Throughout Luke's Gospel, Jesus has been teaching that his salvation is not for good people who think they deserve it but for the worst of sinners (see Luke 5:32; 18:9-14). Nowhere is that more clear than when we meditate on the reality that when Jesus died, he died for the very people that wanted him dead (see Romans 5:7-8)—people just like you and me.

In the end the hatred of the crowd shows us our guilt, but it also shows us the love of God, which secures our forgiveness. Horatius Bonar, a 19th-century Scottish pastor, wrote a poem about this event that helps us to meditate on our great salvation:

I see the crowd in Pilate's hall,
their furious cries I hear;
their shouts of "Crucify!" appall,
their curses fill mine ear.
And of that shouting multitude
I feel that I am one,
and in that din of voices rude
I recognize my own.

I see the scourgers rend the flesh
of God's belovèd Son;
and as they smite I feel afresh
that I of them am one.
Around the Cross the throng I see
that mock the Sufferer's groan,
yet still my voice it seems to be,
as if I mocked alone.

'Twas I that shed that sacred Blood,
I nailed him to the Tree,
I crucified the Christ of God,
I joined the mockery.
Yet not the less that Blood avails
to cleanse me from sin,
and not the less that Cross prevails
to give me peace within.

Questions for reflection

1. In what ways do you find yourself acting like Pilate—doing what is easy rather than what is right? What will change?

2. How does standing in Barabbas' shoes cause you to marvel at Jesus?

3. "Of that shouting multitude I feel that I am one." Is this something you feel about yourself; and how will you let that drive you toward Christ-worship rather than self-recrimination?

PART TWO

As in **verse 26** Jesus is led down the road to his crucifixion (the NIV speculates that he was led by "the soldiers," but the Greek text contains no definite **subject**), he is very near to his lowest moment. He has been through a brutal night. On the Mount of Olives he has looked his fate squarely in the eye: he has tasted the cup of God's wrath that he will drink on the cross. He has been betrayed, abandoned, mocked, spat upon, beaten brutally, tried, found innocent, and condemned to death anyway.

John's Gospel tells us that as Jesus was led away he was bearing his own cross (John 19:17), a common practice in those days. The Romans required a condemned man to carry the horizontal piece of the cross, called the *patibulum*, through the streets of the town. It was a method of spreading terror and keeping the people in line, as if to say, "This is what happens to people who oppose Rome!"

But it seems that at some point in the journey Jesus is not able to carry it any further. That's not a surprise, given the ordeal that he has been through. But since there is no point in crucifying someone if you kill them on the way, the guards grab a man named Simon, from Cyrene in North Africa, and make him carry the cross-piece for Jesus. Simon was on his way in from the country on this fateful day (Luke **23:26**), presumably minding his own business, when he was suddenly pressed into service.

We may be tempted to pity Simon, conscripted into such work through no fault of his own. But in God's providence, Simon was blessed to have a close-up insider's view of this most amazing event. It seems in fact that he became a follower of Christ, for the way that Luke refers to him seems to indicate that he was a man who was known to his readers (his sons certainly were known in the early church—see Mark 15:21).

Walking to Death

As Jesus labored down the path to the cross, a great crowd followed after him (Luke **23:27**). Presumably these were some of the same people who had just been clamoring for his death before Pilate a few minutes previously, and now they were heading out to observe the gruesome spectacle. But Luke mentions that there was also a group of women who were following along, mourning and lamenting for him.

It is worth highlighting the very positive role that women play in Luke's narrative. Women occupied an honored place in the gospel narratives and in the early church, and while the Bible teaches that each gender has distinct roles to play in the home and in the church (e.g. Ephesians 5:22-28), it never portrays women as second-class citizens or anything less than essential parts of the body of Christ. Here, when the crowds have turned on Jesus and the great disciple Peter has denied him, it is a group of women who possess the love and courage to stay with him until the very end.

As this group of women walk along the road, Jesus tells them not to weep for him, but to weep for themselves and their children (Luke **23:28**). There is obviously plenty to mourn over in all of these events, and the women's tears are a beautiful product of loyal compassion (see Zechariah 12:10). But Jesus tells them that they should be weeping for themselves because awful days are coming for them. The fall of Jerusalem will be so terrible that the social stigma of barrenness will be preferable to enduring this ordeal while trying to care for a child (Luke **23:29**; see 21:23).

In **23:30** Jesus quotes to the women from Hosea 10:8, a prophecy that had been realized when the Assyrian armies overran the **northern kingdom of Israel** in the years leading up to 722 BC. In a similar way, Jerusalem will be destroyed with cruelty and violence. That makes sense in light of Luke **23:31**, which seems to be a proverb that means either something like, *If the Romans do this to me, who is innocent, how much worse will it be when they come for you who are sinners?* or, *If God allows this to happen to his beloved Son, how* *much worse will it be for you?* These are questions the force of whose answers it is well worth us pondering.

Father, Forgive Them

Luke's account of the crucifixion is very terse; he simply relates that Jesus was crucified between two criminals at "the place called the Skull" (**v 33**). There are no descriptions of the gruesome details of crucifixion, but instead Luke focuses on three specific details that show how the events surrounding Jesus' crucifixion served to fulfill Old Testament prophecy:

- First, in **verse 32** Jesus is crucified between two criminals; he is literally "with the transgressors" in fulfillment of Isaiah 53:12 (see Luke 22:37).

- Second, in **23:34** the soldiers cast lots to divide Jesus' garments in fulfillment of Psalm 22:18.

- Third, in Luke **23:35-36** the crowd gathers around Jesus to taunt him. In **verse 35**, the rulers of the people come up to scoff at him. In **verse 36**, the soldiers jump in, mocking him with their words and with an offer of vinegar to quench his thirst. All of this fulfilled the words of Psalms 22:7-8 and 16-17.

Each of these fulfillments serves as a reminder that God had been speaking about the crucifixion of his Son for hundreds of years before these events took place. Jesus didn't just drop out of the sky and begin his ministry; but his story reaches back to the beginning of the Old Testament. All of these things show that God has been at work in history to bring about the forgiveness of his people.

So when Jesus cried out to his Father to forgive his tormentors (Luke **23:34**), he knew that his request would fall upon the ears of a God who desired to be merciful and forgiving. These words from the cross almost defy any further comment; there may be no clearer picture of the beauty of Christ. As Jesus hung on the cross in agony, his concern was for the souls of his tormentors. They had no idea who it was that they were killing, even though they should have known. And so Jesus, seeing that they were heaping up condemnation and damnation for themselves, prayed for their forgiveness, adding that in a sense "they do not know what they are doing."

The terrible irony of the cross is bound up in the sneering comment of the rulers in **verse 35**: "He saved others; let him save himself if he is God's Messiah, the Chosen One." They freely acknowledged that Jesus saved others, that he performed miracles and healings, but they still wouldn't believe in him. But their words were pregnant with unintentional truth. The fact is, Jesus cannot save everyone; there is one person Jesus cannot save. He can either save sinners or he can save himself. He could either have died in your place so that you might go free or he could have saved himself and left you to perish. Jesus did not respond to the soldiers' taunt in **verse 37** ("If you are the king of the Jews, save yourself") because he was focused on saving others. Because he was the Messiah, the true King of the Jews—because the sign above his head (**v 38**) was true—he refused to save himself.

The Criminals and Two Futures

The two criminals who were crucified with Jesus were most likely guilty of serious crimes against the state; otherwise they would have received a less brutal sentence. They come to the forefront of the action in **verse 39** as one of the two criminals starts to rail at Jesus, parroting the words of the crowd (**v 35** and **v 37**), and calling on Jesus to save both himself and them. That this man would use his precious last breaths to mock Jesus shows the depth of his depravity and lack of fear of God—a point that the other criminal makes in **verse 40**.

The second criminal saw that while Jesus was an innocent man, it was nothing less than the justice of God that lay behind their suffering; they were being "punished justly," getting what their deeds deserved (**v 41**). It is not clear how much this man understood, but he knew that he was guilty and that Jesus could help him, and so he turned to

Jesus with a plea for mercy and a beautiful expression of faith: "Jesus, remember me when you come into your kingdom" (**v 42**).

Jesus meets his faith with a precious promise: "Today you will be with me in paradise" (**v 43**). This criminal asks for mercy when Jesus comes into his kingdom, and Jesus promises him that he will enter into paradise with him that very same day. What a turn of events for this criminal! He was doubtlessly a hard man, no stranger to poverty and violence. He had been captured by the authorities, kept in an unsanitary prison, beaten for his crimes, and nailed to a cross. And here, in the midst of a gruesome ending to his unpleasant life, he finds himself moments away from paradise—all because of Jesus.

But that amazing promise of paradise is not the best part of this verse. We tend to emphasize the words "in paradise." But really, we should emphasize "with me." The thief would get to be *with Jesus* forever, and being with Jesus is the definition of paradise! The thing that makes paradise so wonderful is the presence of Jesus. It's not primarily paradise because there are a lot of fun things to do and see. It's not paradise primarily because the problems that plague you here on earth are behind you. It's paradise because you will be with Jesus (see Philippians 1:23; 2 Corinthians 5:6). Jesus is the hope of heaven. Jesus is the promise. He is the reward. Isn't that the difference between these two thieves? The first wants Jesus for what he can do for him. He is willing to have Jesus as his Messiah if he meets his demands: *Jesus... get me off this cross.* The second man just wants Jesus.

> The first thief wants Jesus for what he can do for him. The second just wants Jesus.

So ask yourself, could you be happy in heaven, free from suffering and sadness, even if Jesus were not there? What would satisfy you, short of Jesus? What other pleasures are enough that you could be satisfied with them for all eternity? Our highest hope and joy is being with Jesus; nothing else can begin to compare. (To explore this idea more fully, see my book *Passion*, pages 118-120, and John Piper's *God is the Gospel*.)

The Darkness, the Curtain, and the Death

Luke identifies the time as "about noon" (Luke **23:44**), the time when the sun is at its peak and the daylight is the brightest. But instead of bright sunshine, on this day "the sun stopped shining" (**v 45**) and everything was enveloped in three hours of sudden and supernatural pitch black darkness. Darkness is used in Scripture as both a picture of evil (see Luke 22:53; Isaiah 5:20; Ephesians 5:11) and also the judgment of God (see Joel 2:1-2).

If we combine those two streams of meaning, it is easy to see that these three hours of darkness were of huge significance. Here Jesus was swallowed up in darkness. It was the apparent victory of evil. It was a shameful, wicked deed. And at the cross Jesus was experiencing the fierce judgment of God the Father against sin. In this awful darkness the Father placed our sin on Jesus. All of the horror, the fear, the wrath, the punishment that we deserved was concentrated on him and accounted to him in those hours.

When the darkness lifted, we might well have expected that God's judgment would have fallen on the crowd who was killing his Son. But when the light returned, only one person had experienced the wrath of God: the Light of the World, who was plunged into the deep spiritual darkness. Jesus hung there, suspended between heaven and earth, abandoned by his friends, destroyed by his enemies, and punished by his Father.

Luke also relates that at some point during these events, the curtain of the temple was torn in two (Luke **23:45**). The Gospel writers do not specify which of the many curtains in the temple was torn, but the most theologically significant one would be the curtain that kept the people away from the presence of God in the **Most Holy Place** (see

Exodus 26:31-33). Assuming that this is the curtain in question, then the symbolism was clear: because of the death of Christ, the way to God is now open for sinners who had been kept at a distance. The sacrifices of the temple were no longer required for God's people to come into his presence: the final sacrifice had now been offered; sin had been **atoned** for finally (see Hebrews 10:19-20).

And, with his supreme achievement secured, the Messiah, the Son of Man, the Son of God, "breathed his last" (Luke **23:46**). Jesus' life and ministry were marked by a love of both Scripture and prayer, and so it comes as no surprise that his final words were a quotation from the Scripture uttered as a prayer to his Father. Psalm 31 is a hymn of confidence and trust by David in the midst of a great trial, and so Jesus used those words to conclude his suffering: "Father, into your hands I commit my spirit" (Psalm 31:5).

The first interpreter of these events was an unlikely one indeed. The centurion, a Gentile executioner and a member of the army that was oppressing God's people, saw "what had happened" and was led to praise God and declare Jesus' innocence (Luke **23:47**). That is the effect that the crucifixion narrative ought to have on us all. Through Luke's account, we have access to all of the extraordinary things that this solider saw and heard: the conversation with two thieves, Jesus' prayer for his persecutors, the darkness, the tearing of the curtain, and the prayer of committal. Can our response be any less full of praise than the centurion's?

Questions for reflection

1. How does Christ's example in forgiveness challenge you?

2. How does Christ's welcome of the repentant criminal thrill you?

3. How does considering that through faith in him, Christ's final words can be your final words too comfort you?

12. REMEMBER HOW HE TOLD YOU

The events surrounding Jesus' crucifixion may be familiar to us, but you can easily imagine the confusion that they left in the minds of those who "had gathered to witness this sight" (**v 48**). It is not clear exactly what they were expecting (a gory execution, a miracle that touched off a revolution?), but they certainly were not expecting "what took place." The three hours of darkness certainly would have left a lasting impression on the people as they went away mourning—but now the show was over. Only Jesus' followers, including the women who had come with him from Galilee (see 8:1-3), stayed behind to watch what would happen next.

Discipleship When it is Dark

The burial of Jesus was not an afterthought, but an integral part of the larger story. The body that rose from the grave was the same one that was placed in the tomb (albeit a transformed version). If Theophilus is to have certainty about the things he has been taught (1:4), it is essential for Luke to demonstrate that the body of Jesus was in fact placed in the tomb (see the burial's importance in the gospel proclamation in Acts 13:29).

The bodies of executed criminals were not normally treated with much respect by the Roman guards, but Pilate was willing to release the body of Jesus at the request of a man "from the Judean town of Arimathea" named Joseph (**23:50-52**). Joseph was a member of the Sanhedrin, but he was "a good and upright man, who had not consented to their decision and actions" (**v 50-51**). Luke describes him as someone who had been "waiting for the kingdom of God," and so Joseph serves as something of a bookend to the narrative along with the righteous Simeon, who had been "waiting for the consolation of Israel" (2:25). Joseph took the body and placed it in an unused tomb (**23:53**).

Joseph occupies a position of privilege in Luke's narrative, and he serves as an example for us of what courageous discipleship looks like. Up to this point Joseph had kept his loyalty to Jesus a secret for fear of his colleagues (see John 19:38), but he chose the most important moment to identify himself publicly with Jesus (see Luke 9:26). While some others watched from a distance, he moved toward Jesus in an act of devotion and care. God used Joseph's bravery in ways that he could have never imagined, and that donated tomb became the scene of the greatest moment in human history.

Following Jesus may not require of us such a dramatic and public display of courageous loyalty to Jesus (though it may). But perhaps the most instructive thing for us is the love that Joseph showed for Jesus even when it was not clear what good it could possibly accomplish. We cannot know how the Lord might use the faithfulness that we show in something that might seem pointless, like sharing the gospel with a largely disinterested co-worker. The good news is that the God of history is always weaving a marvelous tapestry out of these "small" acts of courageous love, even when we cannot see the larger design.

The First Day

Normally there was an elaborate process for preparing a body for burial using spices and ointments and a linen shroud, but Jesus' body had only received a preliminary wrapping (**23:53**) because that kind of activity was forbidden on the Sabbath (**v 54, 56**). Thus, the faithful women who had been with Jesus (**v 49**) could only note the location of the tomb and go home to prepare the spices (**v 55-56**). Their plan was to wait until after the Sabbath was over and then take their spices to the tomb "very early" the next morning (**24:1**).

When "the first day of the week" (**v 1**) arrived, the women found three amazing things at the burial site. First, the huge stone that sealed the tomb's entrance had been rolled away (**v 2**). Second, there was no body in the tomb to be found (**v 3**). Finally, there were two "men" (**v 4-5**) in shining clothing standing there at the entrance to the tomb. Clearly, these were men in appearance only, for "their clothes gleamed like lightning" (**v 4**—see how Cornelius describes his angelic visitor in Acts 10:30), and the women bowed down before them in fear (Luke **24:5**—this is a common response to the appearance of an angel, see 1:12, 29-30).

Luke's account of the actual resurrection is remarkably spare given its significance in the gospel message; he simply reports the words of the angels: "He is not here; he has risen!" (**24:6**). But it seems that Luke's goal is not so much to interpret the meaning of the resurrection for us, but rather, to establish its reality and historicity on the basis of solid, eyewitness testimony.

This Should be no Surprise!

If you are familiar with these events, it may be difficult to appreciate the degree of surprise that the women felt when they discovered the empty tomb. These women didn't have a lifetime of Easter church services and Easter baskets and Easter eggs creating space in their brains for the resurrection, so when they showed up at the tomb, they were absolutely expecting to find Jesus still in it.

And yet, in truth they shouldn't have been so surprised. The angels that greeted the women told them that they should have expected Jesus not to be among the dead because when he was still with them in Galilee, Jesus had explained that after he was betrayed and crucified, he would be raised from the dead on the third day (**v 6-7**; see 9:22 and 18:31-33). Now, reminded by the angels, they had their moment of realization and "they remembered his words" (**24:8**). All of the pieces finally fell into place like the tumblers in a combination lock; now they understood.

The truths of the Christian faith are not unreasonable, but there are some spiritual realities that cannot be understood by logic and rationality alone. Ever since creation, mankind has needed God to explain the world to them (Genesis 1:28-30); we have never been able to know God unless he speaks to us (in our case, through his word in the Bible). In the same way, the people who encountered the evidence of the empty tomb still required a heavenly explanation. The women who received God's explanation through the angels (Luke **24:5-7**) were able to understand the truth of the resurrection; Peter seems to have had no such assistance and he was left to wonder to himself about the meaning of what had happened (**v 12**).

> Those who encountered the evidence of the empty tomb still required a heavenly explanation.

The substance of the angelic message was an encouragement to the women to remember the words that Jesus had already spoken to them in advance about all that had just happened (**v 6-7**; see 9:22 and 18:32-33). God's word is always true and what he says will happen always comes to pass. The women allowed the seemingly insurmountable circumstances in front of them to overwhelm the memory of what Jesus had told them would happen. What they needed to do most in order to make sense of what had happened was to remember what Jesus had already said (**24:6, 8**). While we are obviously not in the same situation as these women, we too will most likely face times when our lives do not make sense. In these moments, we need to remember the things that Jesus has said to us about what it will mean for us to live as his disciples:

- We will be rejected and insulted on account of our faith—but we are also blessed (6:22-23).

- We are children of God, enjoying his generous rewards, as we love our enemies in the way that he did, and does (6:35).

- We are called to lose our lives for the sake of the gospel—and we will save our eternal lives in so doing (9:24).

- Greatness is found in being "the least" (9:48).

- God gives us the Holy Spirit (11:13).

- Blessing is found in obedience to God's word (11:28).

- We have nothing to fear in death, for we are known and valued by the One who has power over our eternal destiny (12:4-7).

- If we stand publicly for Jesus today, he will stand and affirm us as his subjects on the final day (12:8).

- We have no need to be anxious, for all the riches of God's kingdom have been given to us (12:32).

- Jesus is coming back (12:40)—and we won't miss it (17:22-24).

- The Son of Man's return will bring justice for his people (18:7-8).

- Whatever you give up to follow Christ—and following Christ will mean giving much up—you will receive far more in this life, and infinitely more in the next (18:29-30).

"Remember how he told you..." You can be sure that Jesus has told you everything that you need to know in order to live faithfully in your situation, in your day.

The women are now identified as "Mary Magdalene, Joanna, Mary the mother of James, and the others with them" (**24:10**), and since they were likely known to the early church (see 8:2-3), they could give testimony to the truthfulness of Luke's account. It is easy to imagine how excited these women were to tell everyone the good news that would turn their sadness into celebration, for truly understanding the good news about Jesus will always compel us to tell others. But the reaction of the disciples was like a bucket of cold water being poured on the proceedings: "their words seemed to them like nonsense" (**24:11**). Peter went to investigate for himself (**v 12**), but without the angelic interpreters, he could only wonder to himself about the meaning of "the strips of linen lying by themselves."

You and I are in a different position than the people in Luke's narrative. We stand on the far side of the cross and resurrection; thus it is much easier for us to step back and see how those events fit in with the bigger picture of Jesus' life and teaching. We can see how the ending of the story makes sense of all the parts that came before it and how God was faithful to keep his promises despite seemingly impossible obstacles.

It is helpful to remember this truth when you encounter times and situations in your life where you experience some small taste of what the women and the disciples were feeling. The pain of watching the crucifixion caused them to forget and ignore the promises of the resurrection. And when we feel loss and pain, it can seem impossible to remember and believe God's promises. We are sometimes tempted to believer that God's plan for our life has gone awry, and in those seasons any talk of hope seems like **platitudinous** nonsense us.

In those times, you would do well to remember the resurrection of the Lord Jesus. Remember that trials and problems do not take God by surprise. The darkness of midnight does not mean that dawn is never coming; in fact, the longer the darkness, the closer the dawn. Jesus kept his word to his followers: he suffered, and then he rose just as he said that he would. If he was able to keep that promise, you can be sure that he will keep all of his promises to you.

Questions for reflection

1. What opportunities do you have to be a disciple like Joseph?

2. Reflect on the promises of Jesus highlighted on page 179. Which do you most need to pray for faith in at the moment?

3. *He has risen.* How do those three words change your life and your priorities?

PART TWO

Luke shifts our attention to events that took place that same day, as two disciples were making the seven-mile walk from Jerusalem to Emmaus (**24:13**). They had most likely traveled into the city for the Passover celebration (see their assumption in **verse 18** that their companion had been visiting Jerusalem), but now it was time to return to their hometown. Unsurprisingly "they were talking with each other about everything that had happened" (**v 14**), but well before they arrived at their destination, they were interrupted by a stranger. At least, this man seemed to be a stranger to them for they were prevented from recognizing him (**v 16**), but the reader is let in on the secret—it was "Jesus himself" (**v 15**).

Up to this point Luke has told us that Jesus has been raised from the dead, but we have not seen him "on camera." But now here he is, and it is a little anticlimactic because no one else in the scene recognizes him! This does, however, mean that we are allowed to hear these disciples' unvarnished thoughts about what happened to Jesus. As they explain to this "stranger" the events of the past few days and their reactions to them, we see their hearts as they are, and not as they would like to present them to their Lord.

The stranger's ignorance of what has recently taken place stuns one of the disciples whose name is given as Cleopas (**v 18**). In response to the stranger's question, the travelers inform him that Jesus had been a prophet who spoke with power and backed it up with mighty actions (**v 19**), but that the religious and civil authorities of Israel handed him over to the Romans to be convicted and executed (**v 20**).

The faces of the disciples were downcast (**v 17**), for their hopes that Jesus would be the one to redeem Israel had all been dashed (**v 21**). How could a dead rabbi lead a political or spiritual revolution? They had no more hopes, and now they were left to try and make sense of the strange reports that Jesus' body was not in the tomb (**v 23-24**) and that angels had appeared to say that he was really alive. The irony in this interaction is thick; here they were, having just witnessed the most wonderful events in all of the history of God's dealings with his people, and they were depressed! It is possible to look at the true source of all joy, and yet still not be able to see it.

Jesus corrects the two travelers, telling them that their problem is that they have been slow to believe the prophets (**v 25**). They had failed to understand and believe that the Messiah would "have to suffer these things and then enter his glory" (**v 26**). In one sense, their

> It is possible to look at the true source of all joy, and yet still not be able to see it.

failure to connect the dots is understandable, for nowhere does the Old Testament explicitly connect the Messiah to the idea of suffering:

> "The thought of a suffering Messiah was foreign to pre-Christian Judaism, including first-century Judaism. No canonical Old Testament text, and no pre-Christian Jewish text that we know of, associates suffering with the Messiah … True, the Servant of the Lord texts in Isaiah (esp. 52:13-53:12) depict a suffering righteous one, but the Servant of the Lord is never identified as Messiah, and Judaism never understood Servant of the Lord texts to refer to Messiah."
>
> (Edwards, *The Gospel According to Luke*, page 721)

Yet still, Jesus had been teaching his followers repeatedly that the glorious Son of Man of Daniel was also the suffering servant of Isaiah (Luke 9:22; 18:31-33). And in a like manner, he now teaches these two disciples about "what was said in all the Scriptures concerning himself" (**24:27**). Jesus' claim is extraordinary—*the entire Old Testament is about him* (more on this in a moment).

This is a theme that the Lord Jesus returns to with the disciples in **verses 45-48**. The things that they have witnessed (**v 48**) are the very things that have been written already; they only need Jesus to open their minds to see it (**v 45**). "The Law of Moses, the Prophets and the Psalms" (**v 44**) is shorthand for the entire Old Testament. And Jesus is clear that the entire Old Testament speaks about him, particularly his suffering, resurrection, and the spread of his gospel to all nations (**v 46-47**). We should not take this to mean that Jesus believed that every word in the Old Testament is literally about his death and resurrection, but rather, that every part of the Old Testament pointed forward to or prepared God's people for the King who would come to die and rise again for his people. All of the people and patterns and prophesies of the Old Testament have found their fulfillment in the death and resurrection of Jesus.

This is a strong incentive for us carefully to study the Old Testament. Too often Christians read the Old Testament out of obligation, or neglect it altogether, or see it as a series of morality stories that tell us what to do and what not to do. Every year thousands of New Year's resolutions run aground on the deadly shoals of Leviticus or the genealogies of Chronicles. But if we understand that these books were never meant to be the endpoint of God's revelation, but that they were supposed to show the character and plans of the Lord, culminating in the coming of his Son and the spread of the gospel to all nations, then we will see meaning and purpose on every page of God's word, not merely the New Testament.

The Bible functions a bit like a complex mystery novel. In those books, the first part of the book is full of clues—some obvious, some not. Then, toward the end, the mystery is solved. The clues come together in a way that you (or at least I) would never manage to predict; but once they do come together, it's all obvious! You suddenly realize the point of the seemingly random events that came before. So you can't fully understand the end without the beginning—but you can't confidently understand the beginning without the end.

No wonder the disciples' hearts were burning as Jesus opened the Scriptures for them (**v 32**)! The resurrection makes sense of the whole story of Jesus—really, the story of the whole Bible. The resurrection stamps the word "KEPT" all over the promises of the Old Testament; it makes the terrible events of the crucifixion to be great news and lights up heavy hearts on fire.

Opened Eyes

When the party reached Emmaus, Jesus looked as if he were going to continue down the road (**v 28**). While the two disciples still did not know to whom they were talking, it seems that a bond had formed with their traveling companion, for they "urged him strongly" to stay with them (**v 29**). As they were at the table, Jesus "took bread, gave thanks, broke it and began to give it to them" (**v 30**). The language Luke uses calls to mind two other important meals that revealed Jesus to his followers: the feeding of the 5,000 (see the wording of 9:16) and Jesus' Last Supper with his disciples (see the wording of 22:19). It is ultimately in this breaking of the bread that "their eyes were opened" (**24:31, 35**).

It is probably best not to interpret these events in light of the role that the ordinance of the Lord's Supper plays in displaying Christ to the church (significant as that role may be): as Bock points out,

"there is no wine and nothing is said over the elements … Neither is this is the messianic banquet, though it may anticipate this decisive banquet meal that takes place in the *eschaton* after the gathering of all the saints. The meal simply pictures Jesus as raised and present with his disciples in fellowship."

(*Luke 9:51 –24:53*, page 1919)

Instead, the significance of the moment "when he broke the bread" (**v 35**) seems to be that it was at that point that the disciples were granted the ability to recognize Jesus.

Upon understanding the reality of Jesus' resurrection, Cleopas and his fellow traveler take the same course of action as the women at the tomb did (v 9); they find "the Eleven and those with them" (**v 33**) and declare what they have learned: "It is true! The Lord has risen and has appeared to Simon [Peter]" (**v 34**). The Greek word which is translated as "it is true" is the same word used by the centurion at the cross when he said, "*Surely* this was a righteous man" (23:47). Those two uses represent the essential facts of the gospel: Jesus surely died as a righteous man and truly rose from the dead.

When last we saw Peter, he was on his way from the empty tomb, marveling over what had happened (**24:12**). At some point later in the day, however, Jesus must have appeared to him, for Cleopas and the other disciple are able to report as much in **verse 34**. This early appearance of the risen Christ to Peter is not recorded in any of the gospel accounts, but Paul alludes to it in 1 Corinthians 15:5 (where Peter is called "Cephas"). By including this fact, Luke,

> "corroborates the tradition of the early church, particularly as re-counted by Paul ... that the witness of Jesus' resurrection is ... the apostolic nucleus of the early church, and hence founda-tional Christian dogma."
>
> (Edwards, *The Gospel According to Luke*, page 727)

Peace to You

It is at this point that Jesus "stood among them" (Luke **24:36**), per-haps by the same physical **property** of his resurrection body that al-lowed him to disappear in **verse 31**. The drama at that moment must have been intense; what would Jesus say to his disciples in light of all that had transpired over the past three days? Those first words, "Peace be with you," were a typical greeting, but they are pregnant with meaning. The concept of peace—the Hebrew word is *shalom*—was significant to the Jewish way of thinking; it implied wholeness, harmony, and prosperity. As Cornelius Plantinga puts it:

> "The webbing together of God, humans, and all creation in justice, fulfillment, and delight is what the Hebrew prophets call shalom. We call it peace, but it means far more than mere peace of mind or a ceasefire between enemies. In the Bible, shalom means universal flourishing, wholeness, and delight ... Shalom, in other words, is the way things ought to be."
>
> (*Not the Way It's Supposed To Be—A Breviary of Sin*, page 10)

In a sense, the story of the Bible up until this point can be told through the lens of "peace." When God created the world, it was characterized by peace. Everything in the Garden of Eden flourished. Every relationship was harmonious. Human beings lived at peace with each other, with God, and with the rest of the creation. The world was exactly as it ought to be, exactly as we would want it to be. There was no sorrow, no anxiety, no guilt, and no death. Adam's sin changed all that, however. Sin vandalized the goodness of creation and introduced discord and enmity.

When Jesus entered that closed room, his disciples were "startled and frightened." They were afraid of the religious leaders that had killed their master. They were plagued with guilt for the way they had let Jesus down in his time of suffering. They were troubled and confused by reports that Jesus had been raised from the dead. And now, to make matters worse, they thought they were seeing a ghost (**v 37**)!

So it is significant, and wonderful, that in his very first words he bids them peace. His death and resurrection have achieved this. On the cross, Jesus absorbed the wrath of God against the sins of his people, taking away everything that prevented there being

> In his resurrection, Jesus secured the certain promise that all things would be made new.

peace between God and us. In his bodily resurrection, Jesus secured the certain promise that all things would be made new: that we will one day live in a world of perfect peace and harmony. There will certainly be a day when all of the brokenness and pain that sin has caused will be undone. And his appearance in this room shows that Jesus desires to give this peace, even to failing, flawed followers such as those disciples, and such as us.

As a follower of Jesus, you can begin to live in that peace now even as you look forward to one day living in it fully and perfectly. Because you are now at peace with God, you can handle difficult relationships at work or in your family in a more peaceful manner. After all, if the most important relationship in your life is marked by peace, that is going to mean that you will not be as affected by difficulties in your less important relationships. You may be having a hard day in this world, but you are at peace with the One who made this world!

Of course, this peace must be completely grounded in the reality of Christ's resurrection. If we are to experience the peace, we need to be utterly certain about what really happened when Jesus was actually physically raised from the dead. That seems to be the point that Luke is trying to convey to us in this interaction between Jesus and his disciples. They were slow to believe "because of joy and amazement" (**v 41**); it was almost too good to be true! But in order to prove that he was not a ghost, "he showed them his hands and feet" (**v 40**) and ate a piece of fish in their presence (**v 42-43**).

It is crucially important that you believe that the resurrected Jesus was not a mere spirit or apparition. The bodily resurrection means that Jesus' death really has paid for our sins and defeated our death. If his spirit had been alive but his body had stayed under the power of death, his victory would have been partial, and our future would be partial too. And so his resurrection body means that we can look forward to resurrection bodies too. Paul describes Jesus as "the firstfruits of those who have fallen asleep" with faith in Christ (1 Corinthians 15:20). He is the first part of the harvest: different in timing, but not in type. Jesus has a body that is perfect and eternal; you will too.

Can you see how someone who is certain about the bodily resurrection of Jesus will be able to experience genuine peace in this world? The things that rob us of peace (guilt, painful relationships, physical weakness, death) are all dealt with in the resurrection of Jesus. We have certain forgiveness, a certain confidence that we will receive new resurrection bodies, and a certain future living in God's presence. That is fertile soil in which a peaceful heart can grow!

The End That is a Beginning

Jesus turns his attention to the future in Luke **24:49**, and events unfold very rapidly from that point. He tells the disciples that they should remain in the city until he sends them what the Father has promised: namely, the Holy Spirit, the "power from on high" that will clothe them and empower them for mission. The second volume of Luke's history (the book of Acts) is essentially a record of how this promise unfolds in the life of the church—Jesus sends the Spirit to his people (Acts 2:1-4), they leave the city (Acts 8:1) and the forgiveness of sins is preached to all nations (Luke **24:47**).

At some later point (Acts 1:3 reports that forty days passed between the resurrection and these events), Jesus led the disciples out to the town of Bethany (Luke **24:50**), located on the eastern slope of the Mount of Olives. As he was raising his hands and blessing them, "he left them and was taken up into heaven" (see 9:51 and 22:69). The bodily ascension sets the stage for the next movements in **redemptive history**; having finished his work of salvation (see Hebrews 10:11-12), Jesus is seated at the right hand of the Father, **interceding** for his people (see Romans 8:34) and present with them by his Spirit (see Galatians 4:6). With Jesus enthroned in heaven and the Holy Spirit indwelling the church, the gospel can spread to all nations.

Luke's Gospel began in the temple with news of joy and gladness (1:14), and so it is fitting that the disciples returned to Jerusalem with hearts filled with worship, praise and joy (**24:52-53**). Luke's Gospel began with God entering our world, not to judge us but to take our judgment on himself. He came not for the people who insisted they were good enough to earn God's love, but he came for the weak and sinful. And now he had been raised from the dead and taken up into heaven. No other response other than worship, praise and joy could have been appropriate for those who had witnessed all of these things (**v 48**)—nor is it for us today who, thanks to the Spirit's inspiration of the pen of Luke, know the "certainty of the things [we] have been taught" (1:4).

Questions for reflection

1. For someone to believe in Christ, he must open their eyes—and he can open their eyes. Who is the Spirit prompting you to commit to praying for, that Christ would open their eyes?

2. What part are you going to play in Jesus' mission of commanding repentance from and offering forgiveness to all nations?

3. If you had to sum up the Jesus you meet in Luke's Gospel in five words, what would they be?

GLOSSARY

Abraham: (also called Abram) the ancestor of the nation of Israel, and the man God made a binding agreement (covenant) with. God promised to make his family into a great nation, give them a land, and bring blessing to all nations through one of his descendants (see Genesis 12:1-3).

Adoption: the truth that Christians have been adopted as God's children and heirs (see Romans 8:14-17).

Allegorize: see as symbolically representing something else. An allegory is a story which is a picture of a deeper meaning or truth.

Analogy: a comparison between two things, usually using one of them to explain or clarify the other. So if two things are **analogous**, they are comparable in some way.

Apocalyptic: relating to the apocalypse, a word that means "revealing" and refers to the end times when Jesus will return, as described in most detail in Revelation.

Apostle: a man appointed directly by the risen Christ to teach about him with authority.

Asseveration: declaration.

Atone: to make a way of coming back into friendship with someone.

Charismatic: compelling, charming; the sort of person people want to follow.

Chronologically: events described in the order in which they actually happened.

Circumcised: God told the men among his people in the Old Testament to be circumcised as a way to show physically that they knew and trusted him, and belonged to the people of God (see Genesis 17).

It was also a way of acting out their acknowledgement that if they broke the covenant, they would deserve to be cut off from God and have no descendants.

Consummation: completion; the time after Jesus returns, when his kingdom will be fully and finally established.

Covenant: a binding agreement or promise. The "old covenant" set out how believers in the Old Testament related to God; Jesus established the "new covenant," so believers now relate to God through Jesus' saving death and resurrection.

Cults: mostly religious communities that exercise excessive and unhealthy power over their members.

David: the greatest and godliest of Old Testament Israel's kings.

Demonic: related to demons (evil spiritual beings).

Desolation: complete destruction.

Diligence: careful and persistent work.

Ethical: an action that is right, according to a set of moral principles.

Evangelism: telling non-Christians the gospel of Jesus Christ.

Existentially: relating to existentialism, a school of thought which starts with an "existential crisis"—a crushing realization that life is apparently meaningless.

Exorcism: casting out an evil spirit from a person who appears to be possessed.

Extra-biblical: not in the Bible.

Feast of Unleavened Bread: a week-long festival that followed on from Passover. The Israelites ate no yeast (the substance which makes bread rise) in order to remember the time when God rescued them from slavery in Egypt and when they did not have time to let their bread rise before leaving.

Figuratively: not literally; only symbolically.

Genre: category or type of writing.

Gentile: someone who is not ethnically Jewish.

Gospel: the proclamation that the man Jesus was also God himself, who has come to serve us and to rule us as our King; that he died for sins; that he rose to rule and give new life; that he is reigning in heaven and will return to restore the world. The gospel is good news to be believed, not good advice to be followed.

Hypothetical: an imaginary situation that is realistic, but not real.

Importunate: persistent; not giving up.

Interceding: speaking on someone else's behalf.

John the Baptist: Jesus' relative, and a prophet whose role was to announce that God's chosen King (Christ) would shortly be arriving in Israel, and to call people to turn back to God as their Ruler in preparation for Christ's arrival. See Mark 1:4-8.

Justified: the status of being not guilty, not condemned, completely innocent.

Kingdom of God: life under Jesus Christ's perfect rule. We enter God's kingdom when we turn to his Son, Jesus, in repentance and faith; we will enjoy the kingdom fully when Jesus returns to this world and establishes his kingdom over the whole earth.

Literally: when the meaning is not metaphorical or symbolic; it really happened as it is written.

Literary device: a recognized method of communication in writing (e.g. hyperbole, flashback).

Mammon: derived from a Greek word meaning money, wealth, or riches.

Messiah: Christ, the anointed one. In the Old Testament, God promised that the Messiah would come to rescue and rule his people.

Metaphor: an image which is used to explain something, but which is not to be taken literally (e.g. "The news was a dagger to his heart").

Mitigated: make less severe.

Most Holy Place: the innermost room in the Jerusalem Temple where the Ark of the Covenant was kept and God dwelt in all his awesome holiness. Because people are sinful, only the high priest could enter this room, and only once a year.

Northern kingdom of Israel: because the Kings of Israel did not obey God, God caused the nation to be split into two (1 Kings 12): the larger northern kingdom (sometimes called "Israel") and the smaller southern kingdom (sometimes called "Judah"), where Jerusalem was located.

Obliquely: indirectly.

Parables: memorable stories told to illustrate a truth about Jesus and / or his kingdom.

Paradox: two true statements that seem to be contradictory, but aren't.

Passover: a Jewish festival celebrating the event recorded in the book of Exodus when God rescued his people from slavery in Egypt through sending plagues. The final plague was the death of the firstborn in every family, which could be avoided only by killing a lamb in the first-born's place so that God's judgment would "pass over" that household (see Exodus 12 – 13).

Patriarchs: the "first fathers" of Israel, to whom God gave his promises—Abraham, Isaac and Jacob.

Petition: appeal or request.

Pharisee: leaders of a first-century Jewish sect who were extremely strict about keeping God's law, and who added extra laws around God's law to ensure that they wouldn't break it. They tended to focus on external acts of obedience.

Piety: religious good deeds.

Platitudinous: platitudes are empty phrases that are so over-used that they have come to lack any real meaning.

Plea-bargain: where someone accused of a crime pleads guilty in exchange for a less severe sentence.

Poll tax: a tax which every person must pay at the same rate, regardless of their income or property.

Professing believers: people who claim to be (i.e. profess to be) a Christian.

Property: characteristic or attribute.

Rabbi: a Jewish religious teacher.

Rationalists: people who think that our beliefs about the world around us can and should be based only on reason and scientific knowledge, not on emotions or experience (or, indeed, the Bible).

Redemption: the act of freeing or releasing someone; buying someone back for a price. Although a believer's soul is redeemed when they turn to trust in Christ's death and resurrection, the redemption/rescue of our physical bodies will not happen until his return.

Redemptive history: the process throughout history by which God has and will rescue his people from sin to live in relationship with him forever.

Reverse psychology: persuading someone to do what you really want by asking them to do the opposite.

Rhetorically: a rhetorical question is one to which no answer is expected.

Sacrifices: in pagan religion, sacrifices were made to appease the anger and so win the favor of, or earn blessing from, a deity. Within Israel, sacrifices were a God-given way for the people to maintain their covenant relationship with the Lord.

Sadducees: a religious group within Judaism who were the ruling elite in Jesus' day. They did not believe in life after death.

Samaritan: people from the region of Samaria; a people group with mixed Jewish-pagan ancestry and religion.

Simeon: an old man who met the infant Jesus in the temple and prophesied about him (see Luke 2:22-35).

Spurious: something that isn't what it appears to be, but rather is false or fake, and is therefore useless or invalid.

Subject: the "subject" of a sentence is the person or thing who is doing the action described in the sentence.

Synagogue: local place of worship, prayer and teaching for Jewish people.

Temple: the center of life and worship for God's people in the Old Testament. Located in Jerusalem.

Tense: the tense of a sentence indicates whether it happened in the past (e.g. Simon *ate* the cake), the present (e.g. Simon *is eating* the cake), or the future (e.g. Simon *will eat* the cake).

Theological: theology is the study of what is true about God.

Torah: the five books of Moses in the Jewish Scriptures (i.e. Genesis, Exodus, Leviticus, Numbers and Deuteronomy).

Works-righteousness: the belief that a person's works (i.e. thoughts, words and actions) can bring them into right relationship with God.

Wrath: God's settled, deserved hatred of and anger at sin.

Zealots: a movement which sought to overthrow the Romans, who were occupying Israel.

BIBLIOGRAPHY

■ Craig Blomberg, *Interpreting the Parables* (IVP USA, 1990)

■ Darrell L. Bock, *Luke 9:51 – 24:53* in the Baker Exegetical Commentary on the New Testament Series (Baker Academic, 1994)

■ James Montgomery Boice, *The Parables of Jesus* (Moody, 1983)

■ James R. Edwards, *The Gospel According to Luke* in The Pillar New Testament Commentary Series (Eerdmans, 2015)

■ James R. Edwards, *The Gospel According to Mark* in The Pillar New Testament Commentary Series (Eerdmans, 2002)

■ Jonathan Edwards, *The Works of Jonathan Edwards, Volume One* (Banner of Truth,1995)

■ Wayne Grudem, *Systematic Theology* (Zondervan, 1995)

■ Mike McKinley, *Luke 1–12 For You* (The Good Book Company, 2016)

■ Mike McKinley, *Passion: How Christ's Final Day Changes Your Every Day* (The Good Book Company, 2013)

■ John Piper, *God is the Gospel* (Crossway, 2011)

■ Cornelius Plantinga, Jr., *Not the Way It's Supposed to Be – A Breviary of Sin* (Eerdmans, 1995)

■ Kline R. Snodgrass, *Stories With Intent* (Eerdmans, 2008)

■ R.C. Sproul, *The Holiness of God* (Tyndale, 1998)

■ Geerhard Vos, *The Teachings of Jesus Concerning the Kingdom of God and the Church* (Wipf and Stock, 1998)

Luke for...

Bible-study Groups

Mike McKinley's *Good Book Guide* to Luke 12–24
is the companion to this resource, helping groups of
Christians to explore, discuss and apply Luke's Gospel
together. Eight studies, each including investigation,
apply, getting personal, pray and explore more sections,
take you through the second half of the Gospel.
Includes a concise Leader's Guide at the back.

Daily Devotionals

Explore daily devotional helps you open up the Scriptures and will encourage and equip you in your walk with God. Published as a quarterly booklet, *Explore* is also available as an app, where you can download Mike's notes on Luke, alongside contributions from trusted Bible teachers including Timothy Keller, Mark Dever, Juan Sanchez, Tim Chester and Sam Allberry.

Find out more at:
www.thegoodbook.com/explore

More For You

1 Samuel For You

"As we read this gripping part of Israel's history, we see
  Jesus Christ with fresh color and texture. And we see
  what it means for his people to follow him as King in an
  age that worships personal freedom."

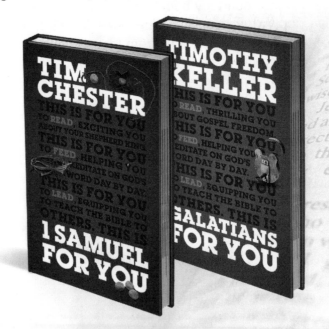

Galatians For You

"The book of Galatians is dynamite. It is an explosion of joy
  and freedom which leaves us enjoying a deep significance,
  security and satisfaction. Why? Because it brings us face
  to face with the gospel—the A to Z of the Christian life."

The Series

Luke 12–24 For You is the thirteenth in the *God's Word For You series*. Other titles are:

- **Exodus For You** *Tim Chester*
- **Judges For You** *Timothy Keller*
- **1 Samuel For You** *Tim Chester*
- **Daniel For You** *David Helm*
- **Romans 1 – 7 For You** *Timothy Keller*
- **Romans 8 – 16 For You** *Timothy Keller*
- **Galatians For You** *Timothy Keller*
- **Ephesians For You** *Richard Coekin*
- **Philippians For You** *Steven Lawson*
- **James For You** *Sam Allberry*
- **1 Peter For You** *Juan Sanchez*

Forthcoming titles include:

- **Micah For You** *Stephen Um*
- **John For You (two volumes)**
  Josh Moody
- **Acts For You (two volumes)**
  Al Mohler
- **Revelation For You** *Tim Chester*

Find out more about these resources at:
www.thegoodbook.com/for-you

Good Book Guides
for groups and individuals

Judges: The flawed and the flawless

Timothy Keller
Senior Pastor, Redeemer Presbyterian Church, Manhattan

Welcome to a time when God's people were deeply flawed, often failing, and struggling to live in a world which worshipped other gods. Our world is not so different—we need Judges to equip us to live for God in our day, and remind us that he is a God of patience and mercy.
Also by Tim Keller: Romans 1–7; Romans 8–16; Galatians

Daniel: Staying strong in a hostile world

David Helm
Lead Pastor, Holy Trinity Church, Chicago

The first half of Daniel is well known and much loved. The second is little read and less understood! David Helm leads groups through the whole book, showing how the truths about God in the second half enabled Daniel and his friends—and will inspire us—to live faithful, courageous lives.

Esther: Royal rescue

Jane McNabb
Chair of the London Women's Convention

The experience of God's people in Esther's day helps us in those moments when we question God's sovereignty, his love, or his faithfulness. Their story reveals that despite appearances, God is in control, and he answers his people's prayers—often in most unexpected ways.

1 Corinthians 1–9: Challenging church

Mark Dever
Senior Pastor of Capitol Hill Baptist Church in
Washington DC and President of 9Marks Ministries

The church in Corinth was full of life, and just as
full of problems. As you read how Paul challenges
these Christians, you'll see how you can
contribute to your own church becoming truly
shaped by the gospel.
Also by Mark Dever: 1 Corinthians 10–16

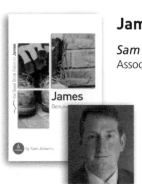

James: Genuine faith

Sam Allberry
Associate Minister, St Mary's Maidenhead, UK

Many Christians long for a deeper, more whole-
hearted Christian life. But what does that look like?
This deeply practical letter was written to show us,
and will reveal how to experience joy in hardships,
patience in suffering and whole-heartedness in how
you speak, act and pray.
Also by Sam Allberry: Man of God; Biblical Manhood

1 Peter: Living well on the way home

Juan Sanchez
Preaching Pastor, High Pointe Baptist Church, Austin, Texas

The Christian life, lived well, is not easy—because
we don't belong in this world. Learn from Peter
how to journey on rather than retreat, and to do
so with joy and hope, rather than gritted teeth.

thegoodbook
COMPANY
Opening up the Bible

At The Good Book Company, we are dedicated to helping Christians and local churches grow. We believe that God's growth process always starts with hearing clearly what he has said to us through his timeless word—the Bible.

Ever since we opened our doors in 1991, we have been striving to produce resources that honor God in the way the Bible is used. We have grown to become an international provider of user-friendly resources to the Christian community, with believers of all backgrounds and denominations using our Bible studies, books, evangelistic resources, DVD-based courses and training events.

We want to equip ordinary Christians to live for Christ day by day, and churches to grow in their knowledge of God, their love for one another, and the effectiveness of their outreach.

Call us for a discussion of your needs or visit one of our local websites for more information on the resources and services we provide.

Your friends at The Good Book Company

NORTH AMERICA    thegoodbook.com   866 244 2165
UK & EUROPE   thegoodbook.co.uk   0333 123 0880
AUSTRALIA   thegoodbook.com.au   (02) 6100 4211
NEW ZEALAND   thegoodbook.co.nz   (+64) 3 343 2463

WWW.CHRISTIANITYEXPLORED.ORG
Our partner site is a great place for those exploring the Christian faith, with a clear explanation of the good news, powerful testimonies and answers to difficult questions.